Christ's
Way of
Reaching
People

Christ's
Way of
Reaching
People

Philip G. Samaan

REVIEW AND HERALD® PUBLISHING ASSOCIATION
HAGERSTOWN, MD 21740

The author assumes full responsibility for the accuracy of all facts and quotations as cited in this book.

This book was
Edited by Gerald Wheeler
Designed by Byron Steele
Cover photo by Dennis Crews
Type set: 11/12 Times Roman

PRINTED IN U.S.A.

97 96 95   10 9 8 7 6 5 4 3

Library of Congress Cataloging-in-Publication Data

Samaan, Philip G.
   Christ's way of reaching people / Philip G. Samaan.
      p.   cm.
   Includes bibliographical references.
   1. Witness bearing (Christianity) 2. Seventh-day Adventists—Membership.
3. Adventists—Membership. 4. Sabbatarians—Membership. I. Title.
BV4520.S25   1991
248.5—dc20   90-19426
                                                                                         CIP

ISBN 0-8280-0603-2

Dedicated

to my two best friends —
my wife, Sherilyn, and my daughter, Marla

Contents

INTRODUCTION

Several years ago I met a graduate psychology student at an American university. After I had chatted with him for a while, he confided to me that many of the psychologists he had studied left him feeling cold, confused, and empty. "I really need to find someone whose approach will help me find meaning and purpose in life," he said, his eyes searching mine. "Have you ever studied a psychologist who gave you a sense of inner satisfaction?" he asked with great intensity.

As I listened to him, I detected a great spiritual hunger, and began to tell him about Jesus. The historical Jesus who lived in our world about 2,000 years ago, and who was thoroughly acquainted with all the intricacies of our human personality. Sensing that I had his close attention, I said, "From my experience and study, I have discovered Him to be the greatest psychologist who ever lived—someone who profoundly understood people like you and me, and someone who filled lives with meaning, genuine love, and fulfillment."

As our conversation continued, I found myself inviting the student to discover Jesus for himself in the accounts of the Gospels. "I sure hope that what you say about Jesus is all true," he finally said, a note of anticipation in his voice. "Since I've already tried for so long to find answers in psychology and philosophy, I might as well check out your Jesus."

I love to study the life of Jesus more than anything else. And

I greatly admire His ability to effectively relate to the people He met. He was certainly the greatest psychologist and communicator who ever lived. Jesus was indeed the ultimate expert in human relations. Who can comprehend the complexities of the human mind and heart better? No one. After all, He is the one who created us in His image, and intricately fashioned our capacity to think, to feel, and to respond.

Therefore, when we consider Christ's example in witnessing, we must realize it is more than ideas, programs, and strategies. It is rather an intimate relationship we have with the person of Christ in which our hearts become entwined with His heart, our minds with His mind, and our actions with His actions. Consequently, we see people around us from His perspective, and treat them as we would Him. By consistently being with Him and becoming more like Him, we acquire from Him skills of relating to others. He, in His person, becomes our motivation, our study, and our strategy. Such a life modeled and empowered by Christ grips the people we come in contact with with the clear realization that we have been with the Master (Acts 4:13).

The apostle Paul utilized two excellent words, *aroma* and *fragrance,* to describe our witness for Christ. He writes that as a result of being the aroma of Christ, God through us diffuses the fragrance of Christ everywhere (2 Cor. 2:14, 15). But how do we spread such aroma and fragrance? We need to remember the principle that we can transmit only those fragrances that permeate and encircle us. So in order for us to ''smell'' sweet like Christ, we must constantly commune with Him so that His character may saturate and envelop our lives. Consequently, everyone who comes into our presence will detect the atmosphere of Christ surrounding us.

Ellen White writes that ''We must individually hear Him speaking to the heart. When every other voice is hushed, and in quietness we wait before Him, the silence of the soul makes more distinct the voice of God. He bids us, 'Be still, and know that I am God' (Psalm 46:10). This is the effectual preparation for all labor for God. Amid the hurrying throng, and the strain of life's intense activities, he who is thus refreshed will be surrounded with an atmosphere of light and peace. . . . His life will breathe out a fragrance, and will reveal a divine power that will reach men's hearts'' (*The Ministry of Healing,* p. 58).

First we will deal with the very heart of witnessing: Christ living in us and expressing Himself through us. So being with Christ goes hand in hand with bearing witness to Him. Jesus affirmed this powerful principle when He said to His disciples: ''And you also are witnesses, because you have been with me from the beginning'' (John 15:27). Dietrich Bonhoeffer, the great German theologian and martyr who was executed by the Nazis in 1945, wrote, ''When we are called to follow Christ, we are summoned to an exclusive attachment to his person . . . Discipleship means adherence to Christ'' (*The Cost of Discipleship,* p. 63).

Yes, Bonhoeffer knew what it meant to be totally and absolutely devoted to Christ and His service. And we too need to be so attached to Him that we may become like Him in our life and service. For when we abide in Him we walk as He walked (1 John 2:6), we love others as He loved (John 15:12; Eph. 5:2), and have the mind that He possessed (1 Cor. 2:16; Phil. 2:1-8). When we adhere to Christ, ''He will so identify Himself with our thoughts and aims, so blend our hearts and minds into conformity to His will, that when obeying Him we shall be but carrying out our own impulses. The will, refined and sanctified, will find its highest delight in doing His service'' (*The Desire of Ages,* p. 668).

CHAPTER

ONE

———

CHRIST IN US

One summer I worked as a literature evangelist in several rural
towns in Idaho. The first few weeks were dreary and
dreadful as I, an insecure college sophomore, tried to peddle
Christian books to total strangers. One incident that hot summer
still lingers in my mind. Alone, and far from anyone I knew, I
took off one morning in my beat-up VW bug to work in a
particular small town.

Somehow I could not force myself to leave the safety of my
car to start knocking on doors. Consequently, I ended up driving
up and down the main and only street so many times that the
people of the town became quite suspicious and called the police
to have them check me out. Investigating, and trying to understand my predicament, the sheriff let me go with the firm
admonition "Young man, make up your mind! Either start
working, or else get out of town!"

Heeding his counsel, I sped to my motel room and the refuge
of its four walls. There I painfully reflected on my experiences so
far and sensed my intense need for God's help. Yes, I was
acquainted with various ways of approaching people, yet I lacked
the assurance of Christ's presence and power in my life. Until
then it had been easy for me to talk about and theoretically
envision His presence in my life, but why did I now fail to
experience it out in the real world where it really mattered?

Something happened that morning that turned my summer experience around and profoundly affected my witness. With my Bible opened to Isaiah 41:10—"Fear not, for I am with you, be not dismayed, for I am your God; I will strengthen you, I will help you, I will uphold you with my victorious right hand"—I spent a long time praying, studying, and meditating. As I pondered the passage and projected myself into every word of it, I took it to heart as if it were addressed to me personally. Its promise became my very own as I filled my mind with the fact that God was the same as ever. And that He was indeed there with me, doing His utmost best to help me and uphold me with His power.

I left my hotel room a changed person. Yes, Jesus was there in my life, and He had been eager to walk with me and speak through me that morning. But I had not sought Him with all my heart. That is the secret of a vibrant Christian life, and successful witnessing: intimate and consistent communion with Jesus. There is no other way. "Watch out world, here come Jesus and Philip together!" I remember saying to myself as I drove back to that same small town I had left in fear two hours earlier.

Such a daily spiritual experience with Jesus constitutes the very core of witnessing, and without it we are representing ourselves, not Him. Our focus shifts from Him to self. As a result we become preoccupied with our own fears and inadequacies. "Personal effort for others should be preceded by much secret prayer . . . Before communicating with men, commune with Christ . . . Let your life be knit by hidden links to the life of Jesus" (*Christ's Object Lessons,* p. 149).

Because "if we come to Him in faith, He will speak His mysteries to us personally." And "Our hearts will often burn within us as One draws nigh to commune with us as He did with Enoch" (*The Desire of Ages,* p. 668). We must saturate our minds with Christ and what He can do, so that we may see ourselves and our witness to others in the right perspective. The challenges we face remain the same, but it is amazing how different they look when seen from Christ's viewpoint. Why? Because He is with us, and with Him we can brave any situation.

Ellen G. White declares in *Steps to Christ:* "Consecrate

yourself to God in the morning; make this your very first work. Let your prayer be, 'Take me, O Lord, as wholly Thine. I lay all my plans at Thy feet. Use me today in Thy service. Abide with me, and let all my work be wrought in Thee.' This is a daily matter. Each morning consecrate yourself to God for that day. Surrender all your plans to Him, to be carried out or given up as His providence shall indicate. Thus day by day you may be giving your life into the hands of God'' (p. 70). Then she proceeds to show how such daily spiritual communion with Christ makes a radical difference in one's life and service. "Your hope is not in yourself; it is in Christ. Your weakness is united to His strength, your ignorance to His wisdom, your frailty to His enduring might. So you are not to look to yourself, not to let the mind dwell upon self, but look to Christ'' (*ibid.*).

Each morning as I submit myself to Christ, making myself available to His service for that day, I am assured anew of His presence and power. I pray that from among the people I will come into contact with that day, He will lead me to one or two persons that I may influence for Him. That is why each new day can be exciting as we anticipate the meaningful encounters God, in His providence, has in store for us.

"Every worker who follows the example of Christ will be prepared to receive and use the power that God has promised to His church for the ripening of earth's harvest. Morning by morning, as the heralds of the gospel kneel before the Lord and renew their vows of consecration to Him, He will grant them the presence of His Spirit. . . . As they go forth to the day's duties, they have the assurance that the unseen agency of the Holy Spirit enables them to be 'laborers together with God' '' (*The Acts of the Apostles,* p. 56). But I should warn you that if you do pray such a prayer, making yourself available to God for Him to use to witness to others, you must be prepared to receive His answer.

Ellen White places a great emphasis on the priority of communion with God for effective witnessing. "Nothing is more needed in our work than the practical results of communion with God. . . . His peace in the heart will shine forth in the countenance. It will give to the voice a persuasive power. Communion with God will ennoble the character and the life.

Men will take knowledge of us, as of the first disciples, that we have been with Jesus. This will impart to the worker a power that nothing else can give. Of this power he must not allow himself to be deprived'' (*The Ministry of Healing,* p. 512).

You see, the proper spiritual emphasis keeps us from getting carried away with our programs to the extent that we ignore people. We reach out to others not just to dispense information, but rather to invest ourselves in them as Christ also invests Himself in us. Although the following statement concerns Christian education, it certainly also applies to Christian witnessing. ''It is not the highest work of education to communicate knowledge merely, but to impart that vitalizing energy which is received through the contact of mind with mind and soul with soul. It is only life that can beget life'' (*The Desire of Ages,* p. 250).

Yes, while the task of witnessing is important, it must never come between us and people, and should be the outgrowth of our concern for them. For example, Lawrence Richards lists the different elements of youth outreach in order of importance. He says it is ''Persons involved together in processes supported by programs yielding a distinctive product'' (*Youth Ministry,* p. 39).

True witnessing lets people experience acceptance, affection, and attraction to our Lord. It is Christ in us spreading the fragrance of His life through us (2 Cor. 2:14). As the loving and powerful Jesus lives in us, He expresses Himself freely through us to others. That is the captivating power that grasps and transforms the human heart. ''Without a living faith in Christ as a personal Saviour it is impossible to make our influence felt in a skeptical world. We cannot give to others that which we do not ourselves possess'' (*Thoughts From the Mount of Blessing,* p. 37).

A fundamental part of Christian witnessing involves how we come across to people—how we listen, how we care, and what impact we make on their lives as a consequence of their being around us. It is relating to others, those we rub shoulders with in everyday life in such a way that they clearly sense the love and power of Christ flowing from our lives to theirs. ''When the love of Christ is enshrined in the heart, like sweet fragrance it cannot be hidden. Its holy influence will be felt by all with whom we come in contact'' (*Steps to Christ,* p. 77).

It also follows that whatever fills our inner self cannot help seeping out consciously or unconsciously, surrounding us with an atmosphere that affects whoever enters it. If we are filled with the fragrance of Christ's love, we will exude that same kind of love, but if we are preoccupied with self, naturally self oozes out. No matter what we do, we will influence people in one way or another. The choice will be whether it is for good or bad.

To illustrate what I mean, let us imagine that we and every person we meet carry containers filled to the brim with some sort of drink. Some drinks are refreshing and nourishing, but others are foul and even sickening. As we ''bump'' into each other during our daily activities, we obviously spill on them whatever type of beverage we already have in our containers. The question is, What splashes out of our lives when others interact with us? Does it draw them close to Christ, or does it repulse them away from Him?

I believe that as church members we are saturated with many evangelistic methods and programs. They are all necessary and have their proper place, but they are of no use unless they are grounded in and spring forth from Christ's method of witnessing. For without Christ, the Witness par excellence, witnessing does not exist. All evangelistic activities must center in the person of Christ, who alone knows how to really approach, understand, and persuade people to follow Him.

And that is exactly what Christ invites us to do: ''Follow me, and I will make you fishers of men'' (Matt. 4:19). It is by being with Him that we learn from Him and become like Him. Only by immersing ourselves in His presence will we carry and spread the sweet fragrance of His knowledge everywhere (2 Cor. 2:14). The more we are involved with Christ, the more effectively we witness to others. ''It is in proportion to our own devotion and consecration to Christ that we exert an influence for the blessing and uplifting of mankind'' (*Thoughts From the Mount of Blessing,* p. 37).

The challenge we face in our witness is to avoid being so caught up in the latest evangelistic techniques that we get so engrossed in working for the Lord that we forget the Lord of the work. Otherwise we will overlook the joy of simply being with Him and learning from Him. Jesus, our prime example, had His Father always before Him, empowering Him in His ministry to others. So how can we possibly say we are too busy to be with Him? If He felt the intense need to have a close communion with the Father despite His overwhelming labor for humanity's salvation, what about us feeble human beings!

"In the estimation of the rabbis it was the sum of religion to be always in a bustle of activity. . . . The same dangers still exist. As activity increases and men become successful in doing any work for God, there is danger of trusting to human plans and methods. There is a tendency to pray less, and to have less faith. Like the disciples, we are in danger of losing sight of our dependence on God, and seeking to make a savior of our activity. . . . No other life was ever so crowded with labor and responsibility as was that of Jesus; yet how often He was found in prayer! How constant was His communion with God!'' (*The Desire of Ages,* p. 362).

The greatest possible qualification we can ever have for witnessing is to have Christ live out His life in and through ours. The world longs for those who will reveal His love, power, and compassion. "The world needs today what it needed nineteen hundred years ago—a revelation of Christ" (*The Ministry of Healing,* p. 143). But how do we reveal Christ in practical everyday life? How are we to experience true success in reaching out to people? In other words, how are we to witness like Christ did?

If we are to draw others to God by the power of Christ's love (which is the only way), then we must yield our lives and methods totally to Christ and His method. And if we are to impress those around us with Christ and what He has to offer them, then self must die, and we must hide in Christ who alone is our life (Col. 3:3, 4). We must let Him dim self in order for Christ's life to brightly shine. It is not merely a matter of Christ helping us to live for Him before others, but it is rather Christ Himself living His life in us. Paul had a clear idea of this powerful spiritual reality when he wrote: "For to me to live is

Christ'' and ''I have been crucified with Christ; it is no longer I who live, but Christ who lives in me'' (Phil. 1:21; Gal. 2:20).

It is impossible to overemphasize this spiritual basis for witnessing, for it is absolutely the very heart and essence of all our Christian endeavors. Without it, our best witnessing methods, even Christ's method itself, would undoubtedly become mechanical and self-centered. In other words, we need to be caught up in a passion for Christ and bringing others to Him before we dare get carried away with the programs. We must worship Him as we witness for Him. Roy J. Fish and J. E. Conant describe this spiritual reality as an inward spiritual impulse: ''It is not programs we lack; it is power! . . . It is not the imperative of an external command that sends us after the lost; it is the impulse of an indwelling Presence. . . . Behind all successful work for the lost is an inward spiritual impulse; and behind the impulse is the Holy Spirit who reproduces Christ in us'' (*Every-Member Evangelism for Today,* pp. 74, 75).

—

SALTED BY CHRIST

It seems that now more than ever before, we hear continual complaints about how sick our society is becoming. At every turn people sigh with frustration and helpless resignation at the colossal problems they face. They wonder how to cope with the ever-mushrooming problems of crime, violence, drugs, moral decay, the breakup of the family, AIDS, pollution—to just name a few—that are tearing at the very fabric of our society.

Many react to such complex problems through emotional detachment, thereby hoping to shield themselves from destruction. I recently met a church member who confided that he found himself increasingly retreating from his witnessing activities because "of all the difficult problems I encounter with almost every contact I make." Then he explained: "I used to be involved in Bible studies much more. But not now. Because more and more, I find myself dealing with people's complex personal problems until there rarely is any time left to study the Bible."

More than ever before, I sense my great need for Christ's love, wisdom, and power in my witness. Psychology and the social sciences may help in some ways, but they fail to give real and lasting solutions. Those we can find only in Christ. At the same time, we must not become cynical about our world, because Christ, who cares about each person and who knows all things, has not given up on it. If He hasn't, neither must we.

Of course, we need to temper our idealism with reality when it comes to helping others. But how can we, as Christ's disciples, ever despair when we put our trust in Him? How can we allow ourselves to become cynical when we study the life and ministry of our Master? This is still our Father's world, which He exceedingly loves, and in which He invested the very life of His only Son. God has a lot at stake in our planet, for He "so loved the world that he gave his only Son, that whoever believes in him should not perish but have eternal life" (John 3:16). God loves whomever we meet. So how can we ever give up on people when Jesus offered His life for them!

One way of illustrating our involvement in our troubled world is Christ's proclamation to His disciples, "You are the salt of the earth." As salt permeates and changes the food, so God calls us to infiltrate our world and transform it for Christ.

During Christ's time salt was a valuable commodity. Various cultures used it in place of money. The Latin word *salarium* means salt money, and from it comes the modern word "salary." The Romans sometimes even paid their soldiers' salaries, or "salariums," with it. The familiar expression "he is not worth his salt" means that a person is not productive at his work, and thus not earning or deserving his pay.

Besides its role in trade or salary, people also associated salt with friendship, honor, and loyalty. Even today, groups of Bedouins roaming the deserts of the Middle East will seal a covenant of goodwill with salt. Also Arabs establish a bond of friendship through sharing a salted meal. They will still sometimes use the following expressions to affirm trust and amicability: "He ate salt at my table," or "there is salt between us," meaning that they shared food together and thus accepted each other as trusted friends.

God Himself sealed His alliance with the children of Israel in the wilderness with a "covenant of salt" signifying His unwavering commitment and faithfulness to them (see Num. 18:19). In concluding His Beatitudes in the Sermon on the Mount, Jesus selects the word "salt" to portray the character and mission of His followers. Being "the salt of the earth" (Matt. 5:13)

21

culminates in and results from the attributes of meekness, thirst for righteousness, mercy, purity in heart, peacemaking, and so forth announced in verses 1-12. It embodies all the excellent virtues found in the Beatitudes.

Just as we serve as the "light of the world" (Matt. 5:14) through becoming "light in the Lord" (Eph. 5:8), so we become the salt of the earth in being salted by the Lord. We have no savor except as we unite our lives to Christ. There is absolutely no other way. W. Phillip Keller draws a fitting and a powerful spiritual application from the amazing way sodium and chlorine chemically unite to form sodium chloride, or salt. He concludes that "similarly our lives combined with Christ's life—our humanity combined with His divinity, our spirits combined with His Spirit—become the great force for good in society" (*Salt for Society,* p. 96). What great confidence our Saviour has in us when He announces that we are now the salt of the earth! Wherever Christ declares in His Word that we are something, one must pay close attention.

Salt has long been known for its many characteristics and functions. According to one estimate, humanity employs it in about 14,000 different ways. What uses do salted Christians have in society?

First, salt causes thirst. When we eat foods such as nuts, chips, or crackers, we naturally begin to crave water or some other liquid. Several years ago we invited a friend home for lunch. Just as he rang the doorbell, my wife, Sherilyn, informed me that she had just discovered too late that the main dish was a bit salty. Unfortunately, in the excitement of our visit with our friend, we forgot about the problem. Our animated conversation continued at the dinner table, and as we continued to eat and talk, I guess I became rather thirsty. Absent-mindedly I reached out and drank not only my glass of water but also my friend's! I belatedly realized my mistake when he, glancing at his empty glass, asked for some more water.

As salt makes people thirsty for water, so should we cause people to be thirsty for the Water of Life. But we must remember that we are not that Water—only Christ is. We are simply the salt, the catalyst that entices others to go to the only Source who can satisfy their insatiable spiritual thirst. Has Christ quenched our own spiritual thirst? How do those we encounter each day respond to our witness? Are they drawn toward Jesus, or do we repulse them away from Him?

Perhaps someone has said to you, "I wish I knew the God you know," or "Is God really the kind of person you show Him to be? If He really is, I'd like to commit my life to Him too." Kathy, a Christian young woman attending a public university, once shared with me how she witnessed for Christ on her campus. She decided at the outset of the school year to focus on the young women in her dorm. Daily she prayed for each one on her floor, and sought opportunities to listen and to care, to encourage, and to be a friend. In just a few weeks her genuineness and beautiful Christian character gripped her whole floor, and one by one they would seek her out to share their concerns, and to ask her questions. "Tell me, what makes you what you are?" someone would ask her. "We wish that we had the kind of peace and happiness that you have."

She was a powerhouse for God among her neighbors because she had been salted by Christ. The friendly way she related to them attracted them to Him. They became thirsty for what she had. As a result, several of them committed themselves to the Christ they had seen so clearly in her life. Imagine what great things would happen if we had more salted Christians like Kathy in every school, and in every place of work. People around them would "taste" their lives, and as a result, would want to go to Christ to drink to their hearts' content. It is true that "He who drinks of the living water becomes a fountain of life. The receiver becomes a giver" (*The Ministry of Healing,* p. 102).

We live in a world perishing from spiritual thirst. Multitudes are trying desperately to quench it through pleasure, power, and prestige, but they simply cannot find true satisfaction. Augustine's timeless words in his *Confessions* still ring with this immutable truth as he admits before God, "Thou hast made us for Thyself, and our hearts are restless till they rest in Thee." Where will others turn to find such rest and peace if not to the Water of Life? And who will spur them on their way there if not salted Christians?

CHRIST'S WAY OF REACHING PEOPLE

While flying to Seattle one day, I sat next to a millionaire. As I talked to him, he sensed that I was sincerely interested in what he had to say. After he had shared with me about all the great things he had done and all the interesting places he had visited, I tactfully asked him if all those wonderful things had given him ultimate fulfillment and satisfaction. My question seemed to intrigue him and he sat lost in thought for a moment, then said quietly, with some disappointment in his voice, "I wish I could answer yes." After searching my face as if for some clues to a puzzle, he continued, "You won't believe this, but with all that I have, there is still something important missing, and for the life of me I don't seem to be able to put a finger on it." Continuing to listen, I prayed silently that God would make me that pungent salt to cause my seatmate to become thirsty for the Saviour.

Who else—or what else—can satisfy humanity's deepest longing for meaning and satisfaction? What enduring answers can we present to hurting people without Christ? Human spiritual restlessness indicates man's fundamental rift from his Maker, and his thirst for something beyond himself. People may grope for this "something" in secular humanism, the occult, Eastern religions, and most recently the New Age movement. Keller describes humanity's futile attempts to find it when he observes, "Many of the masses who are mesmerized by the false philosophies of modern men little realize the drab despair of humanism, the utter emptiness of evolutionary philosophy, the dry-as-dust tedium of false teachings that take them nowhere without hope" (Keller, p. 110). Ellen White truly remarks that "No human agent can supply that which will satisfy the hunger and thirst of the soul. . . . We need not seek to quench our thirst at shallow streams; for the great fountain is just above us, of whose abundant waters we may freely drink" (*Thoughts From the Mount of Blessing,* pp. 18, 19).

Second, salt brings out the flavor in the food. It is hard for those of us living in the Western world to appreciate how much salt it would take to make a drab and dreary diet palatable to the millions of poor people around the world. I sometimes hear students gripe about the food served in their school cafeterias. When I hear such litanies, I cannot help comparing our meals with those of some I have visited in other places. People there have cornmeal, cassava, or rice every day—and sometimes not even enough of that. Imagine yourself in their place. It would be almost impossible to swallow such a drab and monotonous diet every day without some precious salt to make it edible.

As we notice people around us barely holding on, it reminds us of Henry Thoreau's famous observation, "The mass of men lead lives of quiet desperation." They try again and again to spice their dreary existence with the temporary thrills of our world, only to be left with a bad taste in the mouth.

A father shared with me recently how he was running out of ideas and activities to keep his two boys from boredom. Totally exhausted, he confessed that he could not think of what to do next. He had sought me out that day because his sons had complained, "Dad, we cannot stand being bored any longer. Can't we do something exciting?" Then they gave him their "ultimatum": "If things don't change around here, we are going out there to live it up and have some fun." The father looked puzzled as he mused, "How can we possibly have an exciting party for them every other day!" He realized that this world's spices would not really keep them happy.

The flavor that the salt brings out in the food symbolizes the vitality, the zest, the hope, and the joy of Christ that salted Christians infuse in a lifeless, hopeless society. Our lives are to inject courage, affirmation, and enthusiasm into others' lives. Ellen White depicts the savor of the salt as representing "the vital power of the Christian—the love of Jesus in the heart, the righteousness of Christ pervading the life" (ibid., p. 36).

People will struggle on against overwhelming odds if they have hope that there really is light at the end of the tunnel. Victor Hugo, the renowned French author, asserted that "man lives by affirmation, even more than by bread." And Mark Twain echoed a similar idea when he said, "I can live for two months on one good compliment."

But what affirmation can we find in this despairing world? How would you feel if there was absolutely no ultimate purpose and meaning in life, no salvation from our human dilemma, no hope beyond the present? William Shakespeare wrote in his play

Macbeth, "Out, out, brief candle! Life's but a walking shadow, a poor player that struts and frets his hour upon the stage and then is heard no more: it is a tale told by an idiot, full of sound and fury, signifying nothing." Happily, his pessimistic philosophy is not true. Christ through His salted human agents provides that ultimate purpose, affirmation, and hope. Keller explains this concept further when he writes that "God's people are realists. We recognize we are in a decadent society. We see corruption and decay everywhere. Yet amid the mayhem our spirits soar in hope. For our confidence is not in the community of man but in the goodness and graciousness of our God. . . . We can look up and see the stars when others only look down and see the mud" (Keller, pp. 111, 112).

Of all people, Christ's followers should be the most affirming, zestful, and joyous in this world—we have good reason to be. On the other hand, to be long-faced, critical, and pessimistic reveals that the salt in our personal experience has lost its savor. To bring out the flavor in people's lives means to relate to them as Jesus did, that is, to focus on and reinforce what is positive in them. This was Christ's way. "In every human being He discerned infinite possibilities. . . . Looking upon them with hope, He inspired hope. . . . In His presence souls despised and fallen realized that they still were men, and they longed to prove themselves worthy of His regard" (*Education,* p. 80).

Possibly you have had someone warn you to watch out for certain individuals when joining a new church, or when beginning a new job. I have had such experiences. But instead of thinking the worst of such individuals, I tried to think the best of them, and wanted to give them a fresh start. Reaching out to them, I listened to them and treated them with love and respect. I tried to dwell and build on what was positive, and discern their potential for good and growth.

The apostle Paul associated salt with gracious, tasteful words when he wrote, "Let your speech always be gracious, seasoned with salt" (Col. 4:6). But speaking graciously and affirmingly comes hard to many of us because of our critical attitudes toward others. That is why we need to, by God's grace, "cultivate the habit of speaking well of others. Dwell upon the good qualities of those with whom you associate, and see as little as possible of their errors and failings.'' In addition, we must always keep in mind that ''we cannot afford to live on the husks of others' faults or failings. . . . The very act of looking for evil in others develops evil in those who look. By dwelling upon the faults of others, we are changed into the same image'' (*Gospel Workers,* p. 479).

As I affirmed those I had been warned against, I discovered that it brought out the best in them, and soon we became good friends. Those who warned me against such people were not wrong in what they said—generally they were right on target. In fact, they had them figured out quite well. But our primary mission, as salt of people, is not just to determine what people are like, but to interact with them in such a way that we bring out the best in them, not the worst. Even when it comes to our colleagues, we probably overlook all their positive traits. Taking most of their good points for granted, we rarely express our appreciation to them.

However, we swiftly censure and condemn if they falter in some way. And we act as if we have forgotten all the good in them because of one perceived shortcoming. How I wish that we would be more balanced and fair in this important area of human relationships. Yes, we need not ignore their failings, but let us view them in the context of the innumerable and consistent times they have rendered great service. Instead of keeping silent when things are going well and expressing ourselves only when we see that something is going wrong or not to our liking, let us never forget that our mission in this world is a positive, uplifting, and saving one.

One time while visiting a school, I had the privilege of spending some time in the office of an elderly teacher. As I listened to her tell about her long years of devoted service, her words moved me. Suddenly I blurted out, ''I, for one, greatly appreciate the love you have given all these many years to our young people.''

With tears of gratitude welling up in her eyes, she replied, ''Thank you! You're one of the very few who ever took time to visit with me and express thanks.''

We live in a world that is, in many ways, not only spiritually bland and tasteless but often bitter. My parents would use salt to cure the bitter-tasting olives they picked from our olive grove. The transformation always amazed me. From something bitter to something better. Salt can take something as bitter as green olives and transform them into a food with a good flavor. That is precisely the transforming impact that Jesus wants us to have on our world. As salt of the world, let us make a bitter world a better one.

Someone might say that we need only to proclaim the content of the Gospel and not worry about the form of its presentation. The what, but not the how. However, flavor is something positive, something attractive and appealing. Therefore, our mission as salt is to present Christ's gospel in such an inviting and enticing manner that people find themselves compelled by it. It was Jesus' way, and the way He wants us to follow. "His blessings He presents in the most alluring terms. He is not content merely to announce these blessings; He presents them in the most attractive way, to excite a desire to possess them" (*The Desire of Ages,* p. 826).

Third, salt melts ice. During the winter we sprinkle it on icy sidewalks to thaw the accumulated ice, thus making them safer. As the salt particles come in contact with the ice, it is almost as if they generate warmth, thereby melting the cold ice. In the same way, if the fire of Christ's love burns brightly in our lives, then "soon all those around can warm up in its glowing," to use the words of a familiar chorus. In commenting on Matthew 5:13, Ellen White alludes to the spiritual warmth we transmit all around us as the salt of people. She writes: "We shall come close to them till their hearts are warmed by our unselfish interest and love. The sincere believers diffuse vital energy, which is penetrating and imparts new moral power to the souls for whom they labor" (*Thoughts From the Mount of Blessing,* p. 36).

We live in a world that is often cold, unfeeling, and indifferent. No wonder that when we show genuine love and caring toward others without any strings attached, it startles and pleasantly surprises them. However, the world by no means has a monopoly on coldness. Even some churches are cold. But how can that be? Christ is certainly a warm and effusive person. He cannot possibly reside in our lives without expressing His warmth and love through us. Thus, when we encounter a cold Christian and when we step into a cold church, we cannot help sensing that Christ is not abiding in the heart.

If we are not warming this ice-cold, dying world back to life, then it is freezing us to death. Once I passed by an old broken-down house with the roof and some walls gone. Stepping inside from the frigid wind, I noticed that everything looked weathered and shabby except the brick fireplace standing prominently in a corner of what used to be the living room. As I approached the fireplace, I noticed its good state of preservation. The hearth still had some logs stacked on it. But ice had formed all over the fireplace.

That is how it is with cold Christians and churches. The fireplace of our lives looks good with a solid chimney and plenty of wood stacked inside, but without the fires of Christ's love ignited in our hearts we remain cold and lifeless. And the result is devastating because of the letdown others experience when they rightly expect to find Christian love and warmth in us—we who claim to be the followers of Christ—but regrettably discover it missing. They quickly realize that we are only facades lacking the internal fire. "A cold, sunless religion never draws souls to Christ. It drives them away from Him, into the nets that Satan has spread for the feet of the straying" (*Gospel Workers,* p. 478). May the fire of His love melt the coldness in our own hearts and homes, and thus kindled by Him, we may thaw the iciness in those about us.

Fourth, salt brings healing. During Christ's time salt frequently provided a convenient and effective remedy against infection. As moderns, we do not appreciate the medicinal value of common salt. Why bother with it when we have pharmacies and drugstores well stocked with an infinite number of all sorts of drugs?

As a child growing up near the shores of the Mediterranean Sea, I learned about the effectiveness of its salty water against festering cuts and bruises. Long hours of swimming in the sea would apparently hasten the healing process. Even today we recognize the benefits of gargling with a warm salt solution to ward off colds and sore throats.

The badly wounded passengers of the ship *Athenia* survived during World War II because they drenched themselves regularly in saltwater. Charles Bowen, the man in charge of their rescue, ordered the treatment following the attack by German U-boats. Having run out of medical supplies, he had to resort to other means of caring for the injured. Not one passenger died, however, and Bowen received credit for saving them with the saltwater (see Keller, pp. 116, 117).

We see so much hurt and brokenness around us, so many people injured in life's struggles. You can hardly listen to anyone these days without quickly learning about the tough times he is trying to cope with. People wrestle with distrust, depression, despair, callousness, betrayal, and fragmentation, and succumb to broken dreams and dashed hopes. It constantly amazes me how people can sustain so many punishing blows. And it does not involve just the unchurched—church members increasingly face such overwhelming problems. That is why Christian witnessing does not limit itself to nonbelievers, but rather reaches out to anyone we meet along the way who may need the love that Christ manifests in our lives.

The church ought to be a refuge where hurt persons find healing and restoration in Christ and His people. The ministry of Christ is to be our ministry, for the Father has entrusted us with the same responsibility He gave to His Son—the ministry of reconciliation to a broken world (see 2 Cor. 5:18-20). Furthermore, Christ described His mission to humanity by declaring, "The Lord has anointed me to bring good tidings to the afflicted; he has sent me to bind up the brokenhearted, to proclaim liberty to the captives, and the opening of the prison to those who are bound" (Isa. 61:1).

That is why I like the saying that the church is a hospital for sinners, not a museum for saints. Can you imagine a patient being admitted to a well-staffed and well-equipped hospital, yet have no one treat him? Talk to any physician or nurse, and he or she would tell you that from the moment an ill person enters the hospital, it harnesses all its resources to get the patient well. His anticipated recovery becomes its top priority. Indeed, a hospital exists solely for that purpose.

What about the church? Is it really a hospital for the bruised and broken? Are all our energies channeled toward their spiritual recovery? Why is it that sometimes we do not reach out even to our own church members with affirmation and healing? They may even stay in church with us for years without experiencing spiritual improvement and recovery. And then they sometimes leave it without experiencing that genuine love we so often talk about—love that manifests itself to them in concrete deeds of kindness and friendliness. Jesus said, "By this all men will know that you are my disciples, if you have love for one another" (John 13:35). "The Saviour has given His precious life in order to establish a church capable of ministering to the suffering, the sorrowful, and the tempted" (*The Ministry of Healing,* p. 106).

Recent surveys conducted by Roger Dudley and Harold West to determine why some Seventh-day Adventists leave their church clearly show that the reason cited most often involved how the church treated them (Monte Sahlin, "Where Are Our Missing Members?" *Adventist Review,* May 4, 1989, p. 19). An article entitled "The Missing Tell Us Why" printed a moving and anonymous letter by one who left the Adventist Church. She wrote, "For the most part, I was a nameless, unnoticed face. . .. The church can be doctrinally pure, but please, please, let that doctrine be richly enshrined in a love that manifests itself in welcoming smiles, warm handshakes, follow-up, and friend-ships" (William G. Johnsson, in *Adventist Review,* Sept. 7, 1989, p. 10).

We could cite many other functions of salt that illustrate Christian witnessing. Some of them we will allude to in the following chapters. Jesus used a symbol packed with meaning to describe His influence through us in this world! Without fanfare, salt quietly takes the initiative, penetrating, pervading. As it is sprinkled on the food and not vice versa, so we must take the initiative in reaching out to a world that so desperately needs Christ.

To a world that is athirst, let us offer the Water of Life. To a drab and tasteless world, let us bring out flavor, zest, and

31

vitality. To an indifferent and cold world, let us transmit the warmth of Christ's love. And to a hurting and broken world, let us offer healing and restoration. Let us be salted by Christ, so that we may salt others. Bonhoeffer asserts that Christ said, "you *are* the salt," and not "you *have* the salt" (*The Cost of Discipleship,* p. 130). Witnessing does not happen by proxy, it is not done by giving something we have, but rather it results from giving ourselves. For we are the salt, and as the salt gives itself, so must we. Indeed, bestowing ourselves in service to others is Christ's great love made tangible. The love of Christ, "cherished in the heart, . . . sweetens the entire life and sheds its blessing upon all around. It is this, and this only, that can make us the salt of the earth" (*Thoughts From the Mount of Blessing,* p. 38).

CHRIST'S METHOD ALONE

When I am invited to conduct witnessing classes, several will usually comment that they will reserve judgment on what I have to present because everything they have heard in the past always eventually fizzled out. Then they add, casting a quizzical look at me, "We sure hope your witnessing program will be different. We hope it will work out."

"I am not going to present my program, or somebody else's," I generally respond. "I am going to present Christ's program! And His alone is guaranteed to give true success."

Rebecca Pippert comments in her book *Out of the Saltshaker* why she feels so much of our witnessing activities is unproductive. "I believe," she writes, "that much of our evangelism is ineffective because we depend too much upon technique and strategy. Evangelism has slipped into the sales department. I am convinced that we must look at Jesus, and the quality of life He calls us to, as a model for what to believe and how to reach out to others" (p. 13).

More precisely, what does Christ's program or method entail? Let me share with you its specifics and how living it can transform and revolutionize one's witness for Christ. Simple yet highly effective, it is a true expression of Christ's character. Transcending time, culture, race, religion, and geography, it has universal appeal. It is indeed Christ's boundless and dependable way of finding a path to the human heart.

Ellen G. White in *The Ministry of Healing* outlines its several steps. She writes: "Christ's method alone will give true success in reaching the people. The Saviour mingled with men as one who desired their good. He showed His sympathy for them, ministered to their needs, and won their confidence. Then He bade them, 'Follow Me' " (p. 143).

Too often we get so distracted by sophisticated witnessing methods that we overlook Christ's simple and commonsense approach. Sad to say, common sense is a rather rare commodity in the highly regimented programs so prevalent today. Too frequently the common thread that runs through them is an emphasis on tasks and end results rather than on people and process. Robert Coleman, professor of evangelism at Asbury Theological Seminary and author of *The Master Plan of Evangelism,* states that Christ's method "has not been disavowed; it has just been ignored. It has been something to remember in venerating the past, but not to be taken seriously as a rule of conduct in the present" (*The Master Plan of Evangelism,* [1980], p. 112).

"We are slow to realize how much we need to understand the teachings of Christ and His methods of labor" (*Counsels to Parents and Teachers,* p. 391). In underscoring the fact that Christ had already chosen His method to finish His work, and that we are not to replace it with anything else, Bonhoeffer said, "Happy are they whose duty is fixed by such a precept, and who are therefore free from the tyranny of their own ideas and calculations" (p. 228).

Christ's program was first and foremost people. He did not start His ministry by publicizing all sorts of activities and meetings geared to reach the world, but He chose what the Jewish leaders described as "uneducated, common men" (Acts 4:13) to reach the crowds. He invested His time, ideas, and efforts in them, equipping them to do His work. And eventually His personality so molded them that even their critics, who accused them of being ignorant, "recognized that they had been with Jesus" (verse 13). Being with Christ, the disciples emulated their Master, embodying His example of witnessing in their lives.

CHRIST'S METHOD ALONE

Robert Coleman, describing Christ's method of witnessing, writes: "Evangelism was lived before them in spirit and in technique. Watching Him they learned what it was all about. He led them to recognize the need inherent in all classes of people, and the best methods of approaching them. They observed how He drew people to Himself; how he won their confidence and inspired their faith; how He opened to them the way of salvation and called them to a decision. . . . His method was so real and practical that it just came naturally" (pp. 78, 79).

Notice how his portrayal of Christ's method of witnessing resembles that depicted by Ellen White earlier in this chapter. Both authors seem to indicate that if we do not persevere in following Christ's example of personal work, we will wind up displacing it with our own programs and institutions. That will choke any genuine love and compassion out of our lives and witness. Ellen White cautions, "Everywhere there is a tendency to substitute the work of organizations for individual effort. Human wisdom tends to consolidation, to centralization, to the building up of great churches and institutions." Then she adds that as a result many "excuse themselves from contact with the world, and their hearts grow cold. They become self-absorbed and unimpressible. Love for God and man dies out of the soul" (*The Ministry of Healing,* p. 147).

Wayne McDill refers to this lack of personal and loving human touch in witnessing as "the missing ingredient." To reinforce his point, he cites a Princeton University research study revealing that 50 percent of those who react unfavorably to church or witnessing would respond positively if approached in the right way. Equating this "right way" with "the missing ingredient," which he specifies as loving human relationships, he states, "the gospel of Christ is not consistent with an evangelism which seeks to ignore or avoid sincere personal relationships." Then he goes on to add that "evangelism will be effective to the extent that it depends on the establishment and cultivation of meaningful relationships" (*Making Friends for Christ,* pp. 13, 14). He explains "meaningful" as "spiritually significant—a reaching out in love, an openness, a sincerity, a concern that is real" (*ibid.,* p. 15).

CHRIST'S WAY OF REACHING PEOPLE

McDill is right. How can we possibly quench the thirst of the human soul if we withhold our love and sympathy? What good are plans and programs devoid of meaningful relationships? People are not machines, gadgetry to be used, or objects to fit into our evangelistic schemes. They know if we genuinely love them or not. God does not view them as objects to manipulate, but as His precious children whom He loves supremely, and in whom He invested the life of His Son. May He possess us so completely that those who associate with us will unmistakably sense that He is there revealing His great love through our lives. That is the only way God can honor our humble efforts, and grant us His success as we fulfill His method of witnessing in our daily lives. Other methods may give us results when viewed from a limited human perspective, but only Christ's method can result in true success. Therefore, any truly successful witnessing endeavor must be founded on, and grow out of, Christ's method. Then with the Saviour ministering through our consecrated lives—our heads, our hearts, and our hands—we become so identified with Him in character and approach that those coming into contact with us will also come in touch with Him.

Jesus becomes the supreme witness as He reveals Himself through our words and deeds. And our degree of true success depends on the extent that we let self decrease in our lives and Him continually increase. "Every worker who deals with souls successfully must come to the work divested of self" (*Testimonies to Ministers,* p. 168). When the salt is mingled with the food, in a sense it loses itself. In doing its work, it dissolves and vanishes. The eater's senses detect only the food and not the salt. In the same way, we must not promote self in any way, but unobtrusively focus both on Christ and on whom we are witnessing to.

The good news is that when we forget self and concentrate on Christ, when we walk and work with Him, we realize that we do not need to worry about success. Rather, we experience a sense of liberation in Him that gives our witness spontaneity and power. "The humblest and poorest of the disciples of Jesus can be a blessing to others. . . . They are not required to weary themselves with anxiety about success" (*Steps to Christ,* p. 83).

I once met an evangelist so burdened with his task that it almost seemed to utterly crush him. Others who worked with him would also become gloomy and despondent. "Friend, please remember that this is the Lord's work, and He is still the one in charge," I said to him one day. "We are to be faithful workers, but how can we ever attract people to Christ in such a morose state!"

Because we are conditioned from childhood to fear failure, we try to prove ourselves by being and looking successful in everything. Consequently, society bases acceptance not so much on just being a person, but rather on accomplishing something, and doing it well. Sometimes we do not even attempt certain things simply because we fear that we might fail. And it is sad to think of all the great things we could have done if we had simply tried.

Naturally, such attitudes get carried over to our witnessing. We often do not witness because we dwell on our inadequacy instead of on Christ's sufficiency. As a result we worry about what to say, what others might think of us, or about being misunderstood or scorned. Wayne McDill detects three categories of fear that we all struggle with in witnessing: (1) the fear of inadequacy; (2) the fear of rejection; and (3) the fear of failure.

Then he goes on to discuss the practical spiritual remedies that the apostle Paul gives in 2 Timothy 1:7 ("God has not given us a spirit of timidity but of power and love and discipline") to fortify us against such fears. (1) God's gift of power will banish the fear of inadequacy; (2) the gift of love will eliminate the fear of rejection; and (3) the gift of discipline removes the fear of failure (pp. 98, 99).

Ellen White clearly stated the fundamental reason for failure among those who witness to others: "They are working for others' good; their duties are pressing, their responsibilities are many, and they allow their labor to crowd out devotion. Communion with God through prayer and a study of His word is neglected. . . . They walk apart from Christ, their life is not pervaded by His grace, and the characteristics of self are revealed. Their service is marred by desire for supremacy, and the harsh, unlovely traits of the unsubdued heart. Here is one of

37

the chief secrets of failure in Christian work" (*Christ's Object Lessons,* p. 52).

We must always keep in mind that our definition of success might be different than God's. In our finite human understanding, what we think of as failure might be success to Him, and what we regard as success might be failure in His eyes. A church member once bemoaned to me her total failure in witnessing. When I asked why she felt that way, she explained with frustration, "I worked so hard for the past five months studying the Bible with this lady, but to no avail." Pressing her to give a more specific explanation, she said with disappointment in her voice, "Well, she decided not to get baptized after all. So I failed, didn't I?"

When I asked her if she had become good friends with the woman, she replied, "Yes, very good friends." Next I inquired if they had learned more about God and the Bible and grown spiritually together. "Not only that," she affirmed, "but my friend accepted Christ in her life for the first time!"

You see, witnessing is a total experience, not a fragmented one focusing only on the end result and ignoring the person and the process. This church member was successful without recognizing it. Winning the woman's trust and becoming good friends with her, she taught her about Christ and the Bible. She led her to accept the Lord, and they both matured spiritually. The church member needed to recognize that the process of witness itself has success and value inherent in it. But that her friend was just not yet ready to join the church in baptism. Maybe later she would make that important decision. Jesus was still doing His best through the church member, and through other people and circumstances, to lead her friend to baptism without undermining the woman's freedom of choice. What more can He or we do?

Daniel Taylor of Bethel College points out that it is not that simple to measure success when it comes to touching other people's lives for Christ. We should not waste our time trying to figure out which individual act produces eternal consequences. "It is impossible to gauge the consequences of any act" whether it be the "casual word of encouragement or condemnation . . ." If we can grasp that fact, "we can be released from the compulsion for temporal accomplishment in the usual sense. We are given a different conception of success" ("The Fear of Insignificance," *Signs of the Times,* November 1989, p. 31).

Taylor illustrates the nature of true success by pointing to Thoreau and Mother Teresa: "Thoreau shows us convincingly that success is, in fact, failure, if it blinds us to our true nature and needs. Only in this light can we understand how a Mother Teresa, who brings God's love to the lowest of low, is more to be envied than a Lee Iacocca; how some servant of God whom none of us knows is more successful than many a great author or entertainer whom we admire" (*ibid.*).

After stating that a great deal of our service will go unrecognized in this world yet will assure us of ultimate success before God, Ellen White explains that "as the world's Redeemer, Christ was constantly confronted with apparent failure. He seemed to do little of the work which He longed to do in uplifting and saving. . . . But He would not be discouraged. . . . He knew that truth would finally triumph in the contest with evil" (*Gospel Workers,* pp. 514, 515).

Then she encourages us to follow our Master's example by not assuming that we have failed when we do not see immediate results. She directs us to take the long look beyond the present situation and to trust God to give us true success. "The life of Christ's disciples is to be like His, a series of uninterrupted victories—not seen to be such here, but recognized as such in the great hereafter" (*ibid.*, p. 515).

Christ's method alone will give true success, the kind of success seen from God's perspective as genuine and imbued with His Spirit. It must become the very heart and lifeblood of any and all evangelistic activity. True and effective witnessing is not so much accomplished by sophisticated programs as through people emptied of self and filled with Christ, who will then pervade such programs with His love and power. "This is the new evangelism we need. It is not better methods, but better men—men who know their Redeemer from something more than hearsay—men who see His vision and feel His passion for the world—men who are willing to be nothing in order that He might be everything —men who want only for Christ to produce His life in and through them according to His own good pleasure'' (Coleman, pp. 113, 114).

In the following chapters we will examine each different step of Christ's method. So in preparation for that, let us look at it again as outlined in *The Ministry of Healing,* p. 143. However, for easy reference we shall divide and organize it into six progressive stages:

1. Christ mingled with others as one desiring their good.
2. Christ sympathized with them.
3. Christ ministered to their needs.
4. Christ won their confidence.
5. Christ invited them to follow Him.
6. Christ promised to make them ''fishers of men'' (as implied in this context, and evident in Matthew 4:19).

And Ellen White assures us that following Christ's example in reaching others will give us ''true success'' because such a method ''accompanied by the power of persuasion, the power of prayer, the power of the love of God'' cannot fail (*The Ministry of Healing,* pp. 143, 144).

THE MINGLING CHRIST

As a youngster I often found myself under conviction to tell others about my faith. Even today I still remember the acute pangs of conscience I felt over shirking my religious duty. When my guilty feelings would build up to unbearable levels every few months or so, I would fearfully venture into some neighborhood to distribute some pamphlets. Quite reserved and painfully shy, I found it extremely painful to meet new people.

When our visitation team huddled to pray for God's help in meeting people, I would pray silently that I would find nobody home. I just wanted to discreetly leave the pamphlet in the door and quietly steal away. One afternoon as I went from door to door I would faintly knock and wait for a few short seconds, leave a pamphlet in the door, and hastily head to the next house.

After I stealthily approached one particular home, I tapped on the door, stuck a pamphlet in a crack, and rushed off. Just then a burly, no-nonsense man, who apparently happened to be close to the door watching me, irately called me back and demanded why I had left so abruptly before he had even had the chance to open the door. I will not mention all that he said, but that did it for me and my witnessing. At that moment I just wanted to hide somewhere, feeling like a total failure.

So when people comment about how natural and outgoing I appear as I witness, I astonish them with experiences similar to those I have just recounted. I have discovered that for Christ to use me in witnessing does not require that I be an extrovert, but that He must transform me by His power and fill me with His love. It definitely takes all types of personalities and gifts to reach all types of individuals. In fact, it is when we develop and utilize our own particular spiritual gifts that Christ can use us most effectively. In other words, we need to express God's love to others in a way that is comfortable for us, and in a style that corresponds to our personalities. "God desires that our praise shall ascend to Him, marked with our own individuality" (*The Ministry of Healing,* p. 100). And "Stand in your God-given personality. Be no other person's shadow. Expect that the Lord will work in and by and through you" (*ibid.,* p. 499).

It is still difficult for me to take the initiative and mingle with others, particularly if I am unfamiliar with them. Always I require some time to warm up to people. I still remember going with a group of college students to witness in a city park. While some of us struggled to just begin a casual conversation with someone, one pushy and fearless student abruptly walked up to a young mother and started to barrage her with personal questions about her life and whether she would be saved or damned were she to die at that moment. We could clearly see that she was getting nervous as she grabbed her two small children and proceeded to leave. Our friend, not wanting his "testimony" to go to waste, pursued her, continuing to pelt her with more questions, and would not leave her alone until she finally took off running.

As he retreated back, he commented that he had done his duty and had certainly given her ample opportunities to respond to God. The problem was that he became so obsessed with his program that he seemed totally insensitive and blind to the person. When we become sensitive to people, we respond to their feelings. They provide us clues as to how to best interact with them. Are they comfortable, or are they uneasy? Are they paying any attention, or are they rejecting what we have to say? It is much better to back off from our witnessing, to keep the door ajar for future contact when a person might be more receptive.

One church member I know of brags about the approach he

uses in meeting people for the first time. In his tactless and misguided zeal, he does not waste time on preliminaries, but instantly gets to the point. He claims that whenever he travels by plane, commutes by bus or subway, or eats at a restaurant, he strives to sit in an area that has empty seats near him. Whenever an unsuspecting person approaches and asks whether the place next to him is saved, he says smilingly, "No, it is not saved, but *I am*. Please sit down, and let me tell you all about it." I am not saying that such a hard-hitting approach never has its place, but why not present the gospel in the best light possible? Doesn't it make us feel cheap to entrap people, coercing them to listen to what we have to say, without first earning the right to be heard?

Such "witnessing" is a flagrant example of using people and loving things. It is essentially saying that the end results justify the means. However, doing the loving thing is not always doing the easy thing. That is why some find themselves using such techniques. It is a lot easier than listening, caring, and investing of themselves in others. Moreover, in our western society many ask whether something is fun to do, rather than whether it is right to do. Of course, mingling with others can be fun and rewarding, but that should not be our main motivation. God's great love for humanity is what must compel us to act. How can salt be "the salt of the earth" if it insulates itself from the earth? And how can light be "the light of the world" if it conceals itself? Both of Christ's examples clearly teach us that we must mingle with the world around us because His life has already salted and kindled our own lives.

Satan subtly counterfeits the Lord's clear commission to us to be the world's salt and light. He keeps us isolated from any involvement with a dying world by cleverly playing on our fears of being contaminated by it. Some, snugly comfortable with their friends in the church, become quite reluctant to mingle with the unchurched for fear that some undesirables might join their "club," and thereby disturb their cozy arrangement.

The devil revels in all of this, because he knows well that our sinful world's only hope rests in the life-giving influence and impact of Christ's involved representatives. He also recognizes that salt does not belong in a saltshaker, and that light must not hide "under a bushel." Therefore he does his utmost to keep them completely contained. By doing so he hopes to achieve a double goal: causing Christians to stagnate, and consequently depriving others of their witness, and thus destroying both groups in the process.

Paul Little writes: "When the Department of Health fears an epidemic of scarlet fever it tries to isolate the germ-carriers. If everyone who has the disease is quarantined the disease won't spread. Similarly, a sure preventive against the spread of the gospel is to isolate the carriers (Christians) from everyone else. The enemy of mankind attempts to do just that by persuading us to clan together and avoid all unnecessary contact with non-Christians, lest we contaminate ourselves" (*How to Give Away Your Faith*, p. 28).

Taking the initiative to mingle with others naturally comes easier to some than to others. I always find it more comfortable to mingle with individuals I encounter in normal daily events. The people we rub shoulders with as we work, shop, bank, and carry out other daily activities. Those we meet along the way. That is not to say that I don't approach some "cold turkey," but taking interest in the ones I happen to see anyway is much more efficient and fruitful. Because we have a point of contact with such individuals, they (and we too) are much less likely to be apprehensive or fearful of each other. Moreover, such initial contacts are more focused and more likely to grow into meaningful relationships, especially when reinforced by frequent interaction.

Just like any other worthwhile activity, reaching out to others can be difficult, especially at the beginning. For example, a couple years ago, using the computer seemed like an impossible task for someone like me who is not technically oriented. Right now as I am composing these words on the screen of my word processor, tapping different keys and manipulating various functions, I cannot help remembering my great initial reluctance. But after practice and persistence, I am now able to operate it and enjoy it at the same time. Think of the first time you tried to swim, or to drive a car. You had to worry about coordinating simultaneously many different things just to barely stay afloat, or not to veer into a ditch. But with patience and practice, those seemingly impossible tasks have become second nature.

People mingle with each other for all kinds of reasons. Often they do so with some ulterior motives rather than altruistic ones. Because so many have been manipulated, used, and exploited by others, we can understand why, when we mingle with them, they assume that we are after something. Isn't this the reason that we hear them probing with such familiar questions as "What is in this for you?" "What are you really after?" "What do you want?" "What is the catch?" "What are you selling?" Such questions betray how wary people have become about being used.

Most of us have had the unfortunate experience of being taken advantage of. It makes us feel betrayed. I once purchased a new car from an exceptionally polite and friendly salesman. But after he finalized the sale, he treated me as if he had never met me in his life, especially when I would bring the car back to be checked. Can it be that we are like this car salesman? We go out of our way to befriend the person we are witnessing to. But when he joins the church, or when we lose hope that he ever will, we drop him like a hot potato.

I will never forget the time when several young people, who previously had acted as if they were too important to ever talk to me, all of a sudden became friendly. At first I was quite pleased with their instantaneous transformation, even though it puzzled me. Eventually I learned that they were trying to win a prize for bringing a certain number of guests to some evangelistic meeting. "Unfortunately, many non-Christians today are suspicious of all Christians because of a previous contact with a friendly religious person who had ulterior motives. Some non-Christians refuse to listen to a single word about our Lord until they're sure we'll be their friends regardless—even if they reject Jesus Christ. We must love each person for himself" (Little, p. 70).

In the first step of Christ's method, He did not just mingle with others, but He did so "as one desiring their good." He reached out to people for their own sake—simply because they were who they were, and because people were His first priority. But how did He do that? He sought access to their hearts in "a

45

way that made them feel the completeness of His identification with their interests and happiness" (*Gospel Workers,* p. 45).

Once I happened to pass through a town where a church leader acquaintance was employed and decided to stop by to see how he was getting along. As I walked into his office, he began to pepper me with questions, curious as to my reason for visiting. "Are you looking for a job?" he quizzed. "Do you need something?" I quickly explained that I was there just for a quick friendly visit—just to greet him and see how he was doing. After chatting for a few minutes, we prayed together, and I could tell that he was pleasantly surprised and deeply appreciative for my genuine gesture toward him. "I am sorry," he apologized, "but it seems that all the people who come to see me usually have some kind of request or problem. I am not used to people dropping in because they care—just to see how I am doing."

Jesus associated with people simply because He loved them, and because He had their best interests at heart. If we are searching for excuses or reasons for reaching out to those around us, we don't have to wait any longer. The biggest reason for taking the initiative is simply because they are people. That is why Jesus came to this world. People were His most important program, not because of their status or accomplishments, but because they were valuable just in themselves.

A number of years ago someone introduced me to a leader holding a high position in the church hierarchy. At first he acted cool and standoffish, then things changed dramatically when he became aware of my own position of leadership. Suddenly he became quite friendly. Although I was still the same person, his perception of my status had changed.

How tragic it is that we, who claim to be the followers of the humble Christ, show such partiality. Jesus said to His disciples, "It shall not be so among you; but whoever would be great among you must be your servant" (Matt. 20:26). And He would say to us today, "In My kingdom, the principle of preference and supremacy has no place. The only greatness is the greatness of humility. The only distinction is found in devotion to the service of others" (*The Desire of Ages,* p. 650).

It seems that people usually mingle with each other only

when they have some kind of excuse or problem. Then they apologize for "bothering" them or "wasting" their time. As a result they tend to view any subsequent relationship in the context of that earlier experience.

One of the greatest needs in our world is for the type of social mingling that Jesus displayed in His life. But we can fill that vacuum because His love floods our lives, and in doing so, we will pleasantly startle people with the realization that there are followers of Christ in this world who love them as He does—for their own sake. Do we realize that we have at our disposal the most awesome power in the whole universe to change the human heart? The enormous power of genuine love! Christ's loving initiative toward the Samaritan woman was so far-reaching that it radically altered not only the course of her life but also that of her people (John 4:1-42).

Usually we react toward people rather than act. We wait for others to take the initiative. If they greet us, we'll say hi to them, and if they ignore us, we'll pay no attention to them. In a sense, then, we forfeit our prerogative to act, thereby letting the actions or inactions of others determine how we will relate to them. Once I saw a poster that declared, "I am me, and you are you. I am not in this world to please you, and you are not in this world to please me. If we happen to meet, that is fine; and if we don't, that is fine too."

Its philosophy left me with an empty feeling. Even animals show more caring than that. The Bible contains numerous references to all the initiatives that Christ takes toward us. A life modeled after His is not a passive one. For the Christian is his "brother's keeper" (Gen. 4:9), and he is to "look not only to his own interests, but also to the interests of others" (Phil. 2:4). Romans 14:7 declares, "None of us lives to himself, and none of us dies to himself."

Each one of us is a catalyst through which God changes our world for the better. Where there is sadness, we diffuse joy; where there is despair, we spread hope; and where there is hatred and alienation, we transmit His love and reconciliation. Insecurity and a sense of inadequacy may make it difficult for us to take the initiative, but as we discover that He is always standing by our side, doing His best to convey His love and truth, our confidence and adequacy in Christ will inevitably grow.

I used to memorize certain questions to ask people in my witnessing activities. But I kept worrying about how to pop them in the right order and at the right time. After I got myself mixed up and embarrassed enough times, I changed my approach. I decided not to have any prepared questions anymore, but just to attentively listen and simply allow the other person to tell me what sort of questions to ask.

Once I visited the library of a public university and sat across the table from a student. After I had been there for a few minutes, my eyes met his, and, pointing to all his notes and textbooks, I asked, "You're probably studying for a test, right?"

"Yes, but I'm not ready for it," he immediately responded.

"What kind of test?" I pursued.

"A biology test, and I just hate biology!"

"Well, I guess we all have to take some courses we don't particularly like," I empathized. "But what is your major?"

"You won't believe it, but it's biology!"

"Why are you majoring in something you dislike so much?"

"Because my parents are pushing me to become a physician."

Being attentive to others allows us not only to ask the right questions, but also to focus attention on their concerns and interests.

In Matthew 5:13 Jesus calls us "the salt of the earth." It goes without saying that salt is sprinkled on the food, and not vice versa! Salt takes the initiative. We would consider it laughable if someone sprinkled food over the salt. How many countless opportunities we miss by not taking the initiative, by not sharing a genuine smile, a firm handshake, an affirming word, a prayer. No one should ever underestimate such small and sincere gestures. They often open wide doors of witnessing opportunities.

But we fail to develop or capitalize on such gestures of friendliness. "Christian sociability is altogether too little cultivated by God's people. . . . Especially should those who have tasted the love of Christ develop their social powers, for in this way they may win souls to the Saviour'' (*Testimonies*, vol. 6, p. 172). Ellen White also admonishes us ''not to renounce social communion. We should not seclude ourselves from others.'' Why? Because ''they will seldom seek us of their own accord,'' and because ''social power, sanctified by the grace of Christ, must be improved in winning souls to the Saviour'' (*The Desire of Ages*, p. 152). That is why we must not take the position that if others are interested in being our friends, then they should show themselves friendly first. Even if they are not friendly, we need to be—and we can turn that situation around with Christ's loving initiative.

Rebecca Manley Pippert observes of those who wait for the non-Christian to make the first advance: ''What an insidious reversal of the biblical command to be salt and light to the world. The rabbit-hole Christian remains insulated and isolated from the world when he is commanded to penetrate it. How can we be the salt of the earth if we never get out of the saltshaker?'' (*Out of the Saltshaker*, p. 124).

The purpose of the salt in the saltshaker is for it to be used, not placed on a shelf to be admired by whomever passes by. It was put there for the sole purpose of being sprinkled on the food, mingled with it, and giving it taste. Ellen White uses the term *mingled* in illustrating this point: ''Salt must be mingled with the substance to which it is added; it must penetrate and infuse in order to preserve. So it is through personal contact and association that men are reached by the saving power of the gospel'' (*Thoughts From the Mount of Blessing*, p. 36).

Then how do we get the salt out of the saltshaker? How do we get the ''fishers of men'' out to fish? And how do we get the ''harvesters'' out there among the ripe fields? Often we look around us and wonder who is out there to be reached for the Lord. People's apparent lack of interest in the gospel may perplex us to the point where we even pray to the Lord to hurry up and get the harvest ready. But notice in Matthew 9:36-38, what Jesus, the expert in harvesting souls, said right after He saw the crowds. He did not ask the disciples to pray for the harvest. Rather He said the harvest was in fact already ''plentiful,'' ready to be gathered in. While we have no problem with the harvest, we do have one with the laborers. So Jesus asked His disciples to "pray therefore the Lord of the harvest to send out laborers into his harvest." They were "few," and there were not enough of them to go around doing the urgent task of harvesting the fields.

The "crowds" that Jesus saw we still find all around us. They are always a ready and abundant harvest. We are not to wait for the harvest to come to us, but we should go to it. But frankly, the people around us do not seem to be all that ready and excited about being gathered into the kingdom of Christ. That may be true on the surface. But if we were to see them as Jesus does, we would understand why they may initially come across as hard and unresponsive.

Their lives may contain difficulties we are totally oblivious to. They may be struggling with challenges that defy human comprehension. Many are thirsting for something our world simply cannot give. And try as they may, nothing can ever quench that thirst in their souls. But if they sense the tangible love of Christ for them expressed in our lives, and if they realize that true peace and ultimate fulfillment—something they desperately long for—is possible in Christ, they might astonish us by their receptiveness.

The Lord of the harvest, the Holy Spirit, and Jesus the paramount witness have always been at work preparing the harvest for us. When we mingle with others, we must do it with the sure conviction that the Triune God has already been convicting their hearts. Nothing can ever be more invigorating than to know that we are never alone in the task of witnessing. Not only is God working with us now to save others, but He has already been doing so, and will continue to work. I remember as a child boasting to my father about all that I had done in helping with the wheat harvest. "Dad, see how hard I worked!" I would brag to him.

"Yes, but remember, son, that the Lord has already done most of the work Himself," he would emphasize. "The Lord has given us the seed, the soil, the rain, the sun, and the miracle of growth."

Steps to Christ, page 28, explains how the Holy Trinity has already been busy influencing the human heart: "The same divine mind that is working upon the things of nature is speaking to the hearts of men, and creating an inexpressible craving for something they have not. The things of the world cannot satisfy their longing. The Spirit of God is pleading with them to seek for those things that alone can give peace and rest. . . . Through influences seen and unseen, our Saviour is constantly at work to attract the minds of men from the unsatisfying pleasures of sin to the infinite blessings that may be theirs in Him.''

Not only does He already thoroughly know the person we are contacting, but He is doing His utmost best to reach out through us to that individual. And it is nothing short of a miracle to actually see the Lord at work through us. After all, it is His divine mission, He is in charge, and we are His faithful apprentices who accompany and learn from Him.

Walking and working with Jesus is the great remedy for fear and inadequacy. ''Fear not, for I am with you, be not dismayed, for I am your God; I will strengthen you, I will help you'' (Isa. 41:10). We become secure in His presence, strong in His strength, and liberated in His love. Sensing His peace, we feel more at ease and have the assurance that with Him things will work out for the good.

I will always remember the time I met Jacques, a French philosophy professor (who claimed to be an atheist) at the Tananarive airport in Madagascar. Sitting across from me in the lobby, he seemed quite aloof. I prayed that the Holy Spirit would help me in approaching him. It was not easy taking such a risk—it almost never is, especially at the beginning. But Jesus was there, and that made it much easier. Speaking in halting French, I greeted him and made some casual comments about the delayed flight (something we had in common, and not an infrequent occurrence in that part of the world).

Taking sincere interest in him and in what he was saying, I noticed that he was becoming more approachable. After I had listened attentively to him for some time, he paused, looked intently at me, and said, ''I am sorry for doing all the talking. I guess your apparent interest in what I was saying egged me on. Now, would you please tell me who you are, and what you do?''

Well, I have to admit that I always like it when I have earned

51

the opportunity to speak. Also, I feel much more confident because I am not in any way pushing myself on anybody. The Holy Spirit had already been at work in Jacques' heart. The Christian's sincere interest and love startles people. Why? Because most of us are so caught up in promoting ourselves, loving things, and using people, that it comes as a pleasant surprise that someone genuinely cares without any ulterior motives.

I shared with this French philosopher my own philosophy on life. When I noticed that he was paying close attention, I said, "I know from personal experience that God is real. My best friend, He is utterly trustworthy, loves unconditionally, satisfies my deepest longings, and gives me real meaning and purpose in life." We dialogued back and forth for a while till we were ready to board the plane, then he turned to me and with seriousness in his voice, commented, "I really wish I could have the kind of faith in God that you have." Then he continued with some hesitation, "Perhaps this is what I am looking for. I am quite surprised that I am actually saying this to you, but I think I am going to look more into it."

Yes, the Holy Spirit takes our simple social contact and humble and sincere testimony, and uses them to soften and convict the most hardened heart. "By being social and coming close to the people, you may turn the current of their thoughts more readily than by the most able discourse" (*Gospel Workers,* p. 193). God has so many providential opportunities to witness that He wants to send our way. And if we are in tune with His great passion to save the lost, and take the initiative, remarkable experiences will happen that would not otherwise.

But to what extent are we to socialize with others? Sometimes we associate too much as well as not at all. Our answer is Christ Himself. Yes, He identified Himself with people, but in order to transform them into His image. For example, we detect the twin elements of identification and transformation in the experience of the woman dragged before Jesus to be stoned (John 8:2-11). Identification: Jesus asked Mary, "Woman, where are they? Has no one condemned you?"

"No one, sir," she answered.

"Then neither do I condemn you," He assured her. But that was not the end of the story. Transformation: His admonition to live a righteous life based on His acceptance of her. "Go now and leave your life of sin."

In such incarnational ministry, we identify with people's needs and feelings, while pointing them to Jesus, who can satisfy their deepest longings. And from being anchored in Him the Rock, from that position of strength, we can reach out to others, identify with them, lift them out of sin's ditch, and set their feet on spiritually higher ground.

We are both in this world and not of it. While we are to change the world, we must not let it transform us (John 17:15, 16). Fish and Conant illustrate this important point when they remind us, "It is all right for the church to be in the world, provided the world is not in the church. The ship does not sink when it is launched into the water; it sinks when the water gets into the ship. . . . The rescue work of the church declines in direct proportion to how much the world invades the church" (*Every-Member Evangelism*, p. 48).

CHAPTER

FIVE

———

THE SYMPATHIZING CHRIST

General Dwight D. Eisenhower had not only earned a reputation for his courage during World War II, but also for the way he dealt with his soldiers. As the supreme commander of the Allied Forces, he often mingled with his troops to give encouragement and support. It is reported that during one of the major offensives launched against the Nazi forces, General Eisenhower was walking near the Rhine River when he ran into a soldier who appeared gloomy and dejected. "How are you feeling, son?" he asked.

"General," the young man replied, "I'm awful nervous."

"Well," Eisenhower said, "you and I are a good pair then, because I feel that way too. Maybe if we just walk along together, we'll be good for each other."

The way Eisenhower related to that depressed soldier illustrates what it means to show sympathy to others. The general listened empathetically, he identified and shared openly his own feelings, and he walked alongside with the young man, not to feel sorry for him, but to be mutually encouraged. The word *sympathy* comes from the Greek *sympatheia,* which stems from two roots, *syn* meaning "together," and *pathos* "feeling." Hence *sympathy* literally means feeling together. Webster defines it as "an entering into, or the ability to enter into, another person's mental state, feelings, emotions, etc."

54

Unfortunately, many misunderstand the significance of sympathy. They think that to sympathize with others is to feel sorry for them, to lower oneself to their level, or to approach them with a sense of superiority and condescension. Thus the word frequently has a negative connotation, as illustrated in such defensive reactions as "I really don't need your sympathy!" In our Western society we want to come across as strong and self-sufficient, and thus reject anything that might suggest weakness and dependency.

Douglas Cooper asserts that "we attach virtue to aloofness. Even in the church, we laud the person who is able to stay unemotional and detached through just about everything" (*Living God's Love,* p. 153). During the funeral of President John F. Kennedy, people admired his widow for remaining strong and stoical, not shedding any tears or showing much emotion. It is really awkward for us to sympathize with people who are weak, handicapped, or hurting in some way. We find ourselves drawn to seemingly happy people and situations, and repelled by those who are suffering. Always striving to have "a good time," we avoid painful circumstances lest they remind us of our own vulnerabilities.

That is why when we hear a terminally ill patient comment that he is going to die, we often respond, "Don't say that! No, you are not going to die. You will just be fine." The patient may desperately be seeking our understanding and sympathy to help him face death. Cooper tells of his uncomfortable experience as a chaplain visiting a young mother dying of cancer. "How a person could fail more miserably at sympathizing I do not know," he wrote later. "Instead of basing my response on her feelings, I based it on my own. What she had shared distressed me, made me uncomfortable. It did not fit my mood. It was unpleasant. I shrank. I could not accept the challenge or get involved. So I ignored it" (*ibid.,* pp. 154, 155).

Once I asked a funeral director why makeup is used on the deceased. He said that they need to have some color, for they look too pale to their loved ones and friends. We say "he passed away," instead of simply stating he died. Once a woman

comforted her friend who had just lost her husband by saying
"He looks good, doesn't he?"

"No, he does not. He looks dead!" the widow exploded.

Even in death we want to fake or gloss over our real situation.
We seem unable or unwilling to deal with unpleasant reality. But
Jesus showed His sympathy with the hurting and the grieving,
and He was not repulsed by human pain and sufferings. He even
used visiting the sick and the imprisoned (situations we easily
shun) as criteria for being ready for His coming (see Matt.
25:36).

At least three other terms are closely associated with the word
sympathy: empathy, compassion, and comfort. *Empathy* comes
from the Greek *empatheia,* which stems from *en* meaning "in,"
and *pathos,* "feeling." Hence the combined literal meaning is
"in feeling." In other words, putting yourself in the place of
another person so that you may understand his or her feelings and
thoughts. Or as we say sometimes, to walk in his shoes.

Compassion comes from the Latin term *compati,* which also
stems from *com,* "with" or "together," and *pati,* "to suffer."
And the combined literal meaning is "suffering with," or
"suffering together." It is sharing the suffering with the victims,
and being passionately moved to help them out of their difficulty.
Professor Harvie M. Conn, of Westminster Theological Seminary, explains what it means to be compassionate. According to
him, compassion should embrace not only the person who
transgresses, but also the one who is transgressed against.
"Compassion is more than maternal tenderness," he asserts,
"more than Pharaoh's daughter seeing the baby Moses crying. It
is Pharaoh's daughter seeing the baby of an oppressed Hebrew
crying (Ex. 2:6). It is tenderness translated into action in behalf
of the sinned against" (Conn, *Evangelism,* p. 45).

The word *compassion* is intimately linked with the ministry
of Jesus. We know that He is the Lord of all compassion, for
when He saw the leper He was "moved with compassion" (Mark
1:40, KJV), and when He observed the widow of Nain mourning
the death of her only son, "he had compassion on her" (Luke
7:13). Encountering the harassed and helpless crowds, again "He
had compassion for them" (Matt. 9:36). The religion of Christ

was not just of the mind but also of the heart. After all, He did die of a broken heart.

Do we sense in our own hearts a similar passion for others? Do we feel in our innermost being a Christlike compassion over lost humanity? John Jowett, known as the greatest preacher during his time, wrote, "The gospel of a broken heart demands the ministry of bleeding hearts. . . . As soon as we cease to bleed, we cease to bless. . . . We can never heal the needs we do not feel" (in George Sweeting, *How to Witness Successfully,* p. 83).

Scripture associates the word *comfort* with Jesus and the Holy Spirit (1 John 2:1; John 14:16). They are both comforters as shown in one important meaning of the Greek word *parakletos.* The word derives from *para,* "beside," and *kletos,* "one called." *Parakletos* is someone who comes to stay close to us. Christ through the Holy Spirit is present with us, and He will never leave or forsake us, but is always there to empathize, encourage, and enable. This concept of comforting is seen clearly in Luke 24:15 when Christ "drew near" to the two disciples and joined them on their journey.

Jesus sympathized with people, and He directed most of His sympathy to individuals. Apparently He did not consider such personal efforts a waste of time. Just as the salt is sprinkled grain by grain, so He poured His sympathy on people as He reached out to them one-to-one. Look at Him talking and sympathizing with a prostitute, a thief, a blind man, a widow, a mother, a child, a young man, a Samaritan woman—and the list goes on. "The work of Christ was largely made up of personal interviews. He had a faithful regard for the one-soul audience" (*Testimonies for the Church,* vol. 6, p. 115).

Often we feel ill at ease when relating to people on an individual basis or in small groups. We are afraid that our masks, which safely conceal our true selves, might drop off a bit and reveal some of our burdens and shortcomings. Or that others might unburden some of their problems on us, which might oblige us to get involved in helping them. Of course that calls for us to take risks and to invest of our time, of our resources, and of ourselves in them. Ellen White said that "the highest missionary work" is accomplished by the "personal labor" of becoming familiar with those around us. "By visiting the people, talking, praying, sympathizing with them, you will win hearts" (*ibid.*, vol. 9, p. 41). Elsewhere she asserts that "in Christlike sympathy we should come close to men individually" for "while logic may fail to move, and argument be powerless to convince, the love of Christ, revealed in personal ministry, may soften the stony heart" (*Christ's Object Lessons,* p. 57).

A man apparently receiving great spiritual blessing from a small Bible fellowship group suddenly dropped out after a few weeks. When I chatted with him later, I mentioned that we all had missed him, then tactfully asked why he had stopped coming. His answer was quite revealing. He confided that while he desperately needed such spiritual fellowship, he was willing to sacrifice it to protect his position and chance of promotion in church leadership. Despite my comment that all of us have our human imperfections, he felt that he had to continue to project his everything-is-all-right image.

I believe that may be the reason that some of us feel more comfortable with large groups such as church potlucks and big churches, where we can get lost in the crowd and not have to get close to individuals. Modern society has depersonalized humanity, including the church, leading to fragmentation, alienation, and constant mobility. Too many of us seem caught up in the mad rush to earn more money to buy more gadgets. Whatever precious time we might have left to develop meaningful personal relationships we squander in front of the TV or VCR, or in other entertainments. As a result, we have diminished our humanity, making us feel sufficient, self-centered, and—locked in our own individual worlds—apathetic and not wanting to be disturbed.

More and more human beings feel like a number lost in a maze of statistics, or a digit tossed in a jungle of red tape. A woman ordered a certain piece of merchandise by mail and, receiving the bill, promptly mailed the company a check for the entire amount. About two months later, to her utter surprise, she received a notice for a past-due bill with an unpaid balance of $00.00. Dutifully she wrote a nice letter of explanation to the company along with proof of full payment, thinking that would be the end of it. Apparently the computerized system did not pay much attention to her letter, for she subsequently received additional dunning notices for several months. When a computer form letter threatened to turn her over to a collection agency, she consulted her attorney who advised her simply to issue a check for the amount due of $00.00 to the company. Although she felt silly, she wrote a check for the amount of zero dollars! After all, what did she have to lose? To her relief, she stopped getting the threatening notices, and she was glad that the company had finally straightened her account out. But it was not over yet. One day she got another notice. After she tore the letter open, she could not believe what she saw. There, under the column of unpaid balance, was a fine of $15 for late payment of her bill!

Perhaps such incidents are not that common, but they do reveal something of how impersonal our society has become in many areas of life. The mechanical way we often treat each other has created a vacuum of human warmth and touch. Humans are not machines, but beings created in God's image who thrive on compassion, sympathy, and love. "Most men and women are not looking for religion," Arthur McPhee writes, "nor do they have the time or inclination to ask themselves questions about the meaning of life. . . . But most men and women are looking for love" (*Friendship Evangelism*, p. 56).

The lack of simple Christian trusting and caring exists not only in the world, but also among church members. Trusting to help us be open and committed, and caring to take genuine interest in the other person. Such personal experience or involvement cannot just be voted or programmed. It can only flow out of a heart that is secure in Christ, and full of His love and sympathy because "the heart of the human problem is the problem of the human heart" (David Watson, *I Believe in Evangelism*, p. 17). Sweeting of the Moody Bible Institute emphasizes that "before evangelism can ever be a program, it must be first a passion." Then he admonishes that "if we are to witness for Christ successfully, we must honestly care for people" (p. 83).

If in the church, the body of Christ, we do not find this love and compassion, then where can we? A major reason why so many people struggle with mental and emotional problems is their unmet need for love. Karl Menninger, the noted American psychiatrist, places greater value on the healing power of love than any other cure. He said that "love is the key to the entire therapeutic program of the modern psychiatric hospital" (in McPhee, p. 56).

The church must be the place where we abundantly find such love and sympathy. Christ, our example, showed His sympathy for people, and His example must pervade our own lives and churches. Persons coming in touch with us must be convinced that there are indeed people in this world who truly emulate Christ in ways they can actually see and experience. Although without the grace of Christ that would be impossible, as our supreme model, He will teach us how.

"He who took humanity upon Himself knows how to sympathize with the sufferings of humanity. Not only does Christ know every soul, and the peculiar needs and trials of that soul, but He knows all the circumstances that chafe and perplex the spirit" (*The Ministry of Healing,* p. 249). Will they find in us a refuge of warmth and sympathy from the coldness and cruelty so prevalent among human relationships? Do we realize that "the inhumanity of man toward man is our greatest sin" (*ibid.,* p. 163)? Oh, how desperately we need to have the sympathizing heart of Christ in our indifferent world!

But what really sets the Christian apart is his genuine sympathy toward others. "True sympathy between man and his fellow man is to be the sign distinguishing those who love and fear God from those who are unmindful of His law" (*Medical Ministry,* p. 251). John Ruskin, the noted English writer, concurs when he explains that "the ennobling difference between one man and another is that one feels more than another."

Ray Stedman shows that the early church utilized two approaches in witnessing to the world: proclamation (*kerygma*) of the good news, and fellowship (*koinonia*) with the believers. The pagans could reject the proclamation as just another idea or philosophy, but they could not easily ignore the tangible results of Christian fellowship. The genuine love and sympathy, which came only from intimately knowing Christ, was so clearly manifested in the Christians' relationships with each other that it provoked a pagan writer to exclaim, "How these Christians love one another!"

Stedman laments the dearth of loving fellowship when he compares the early church with the present one's destructive effects on our spiritual vitality and witness. He states that "the present-day church has managed to do away with *koinonia* almost completely, reducing the witness of the church to proclamation (*kerygma*) alone. It has thus succeeded in doing two things simultaneously: removing the major safeguard to the health of the church from within, and greatly weakening its effective witness before the world without" (*Body Life*, pp. 108, 109).

I believe that Stedman's analysis also applies to our own denomination. While we are definitely a proclaiming church, unfortunately we are not so much a truly fellowshipping church. In fact, sometimes I wonder if we really understand what true Christian fellowship is all about. So conditioned to quickly warn the world of a soon-coming Christ and His impending judgment, we neglect to let others know that we are His disciples by *our love for each other*. The two things must go hand in hand, because they both reinforce each other. For how can we be prepared for Christ's coming, and how can we ready others, unless we experience what a loving fellowship is?

Probably that is the reason why we publicize the successful results in our proclamation ministry but hush up our failure in our fellowship ministry. We broadcast it when new members join the church, but we remain strangely silent when they leave. Why is that? Perhaps the following insightful and sobering statement points us to the answer: "Backsliders, church dropouts, inactive members, whatever we call them, cause us pain. It's the side of our church that we whisper about but find difficult to talk about publicly, for by admitting that backsliders exist, we speak of failure. Whether it's ours or theirs, it's still failure. And failure is hard to swallow in any line, particularly by a church that senses a last-day prophetic calling and wants to be seen as successful, as growing, as friendly, as sharing the true gospel of Christ" (Myron Widmer, "My Friends, the 'Missing,' " *Adventist Review*, May 4, 1989, p. 5).

Without Christ's sympathy in our lives, and without feeling

His compassion, our witness becomes a formality, a duty devoid of warmth, vitality, and power. How greatly we need to follow "the wonderful example of Christ, the matchless tenderness with which He entered into the feelings of others, weeping with those who wept, rejoicing with those who rejoiced." It "must have a deep influence upon the character of all who follow Him in sincerity" (*The Ministry of Healing*, pp. 157, 158).

Each of us must pray for Jesus to transform our stony hearts into hearts of flesh that can feel the sorrows of others, and can be touched and moved by their infirmities. We need more Christlike sympathy that springs from a truly loving heart. May this last-day prediction of Jesus recorded in Matthew 24:12 never be fulfilled among us: "And because wickedness is multiplied, most men's love will grow cold."

While we can show sympathy in many different ways, probably the most powerful way is to attentively and caringly listen. Taking a break from writing this book, I watched a moving example of sympathy on the TV program *60 Minutes* presented by CBS, December 10, 1989. A French television crew had finally received permission from the Soviet authorities to visit and interview some longtime prisoners of conscience.

The prisoners were visibly shocked, yet greatly heartened to know that the outside world had not totally forgotten about them during their terrible ordeal in the gulags. It overwhelmed them when the French interviewers told them that they were there for the sole purpose of listening to anything they wanted to say, that somebody had taken the initiative and the risk to listen to them. One prisoner in particular kept exclaiming, "You are really here to listen to us!"

We do not have to worry (at least for now) about harsh physical imprisonment and deprivation. Yet, even in our free society many lack trusted friends with whom they can feel free to open their hearts. Friends who accept them for who they are, and sympathetically listen to them. It is truly a rare blessing to have such friends nowadays. We know that many tragic suicides would not have taken place if the unfortunate victims had just had one good friend who cared and listened to their hurts.

Someone may say that we only need Christ to listen to and

sympathize with us. That is certainly true, but how could others know about His wonderful qualities unless they see them demonstrated in our lives? How would they know that Christianity works in real-life situations unless they witness it operating in us? In a sense we become the hands of Jesus that touch with compassion, His ears that listen with interest, His heart that overflows with tangible loving acts. When they see, they will believe.

"Following World War I a sculptor offered to restore a damaged statue of Christ that stood in front of a church in Germany. Both hands of the statue had been destroyed. But after considering the matter, the congregation voted to leave the statue without hands to convey the message that Christ depends on our hands to do His work" (George E. Knowles, *How to Help Your Church Grow,* p. 81).

McDill confirms this basic idea when he writes that "the unbeliever will be much more receptive to the idea that God really cares when he has a Christian friend who has demonstrated that godly care." Then he points out that such genuine caring makes great impact because it is least expected, and because it is not at all common in our indifferent world. "In this sense the Christian is himself good news. So few people are around who really care. He is unique, a rare and welcomed oddity in a self-centered world" (*Making Friends for Christ,* pp. 65, 66). How else is it possible to implement the counsel given in Galatians 6:2 to "bear one another's burdens, and so fulfil the law of Christ" unless we sincerely care to know what such burdens are? And how can we possibly know unless we listen, as Jesus does, to what people have to say?

"The law, or principle, that motivated Christ's life was that of bearing others' burdens. Christ came to earth as man's great burden bearer (see Isa. 53:6)" (*The SDA Bible Commentary,* vol. 6, p. 985). Christ could have admonished people with heavy burdens to go to the Father. But He did not. Instead He invited them to come to Him (Matt. 11:28), demonstrating to them what God is like. We too, as His representatives, must follow His example. For His ministry is our ministry (2 Cor. 5:18-20). Participating in such healing and restoration, we are living out

His law of loving others as He has loved us (John 13:34). Others get in touch with Jesus by seeing Him actively at work in our lives.

Naturally, we must recognize that some burdens should be taken to Christ alone, others only to family members and close friends. But that still leaves great room to mutually share many concerns. Keeping this in mind, let us notice carefully what Stedman says in this regard. He asserts that sharing burdens with others "calls for honesty and openness with other Christians, and a mutual recognition that it is neither abnormal nor unspiritual to have burdens and problems in one's Christian experience." Then he proceeds to candidly remark that "somehow the masks have to come off and facades that say 'everything is all right' when everything is anything but right have to be removed" (Stedman, p. 109).

Someone observed that we need to listen twice as much as we talk, because the Lord created us with two ears and just one mouth. Unfortunately with many of us, we not only listen less than we talk, but real listening is almost nonexistent. I know, because I constantly have to remind myself to attentively listen. As I visited young pastors to promote evangelism in their districts, it impressed on my mind the tremendous value of listening. Instead of pushing my programs on them, I let them share freely about their own burdens, challenges, and aspirations. Then I would visit their wives and children. Frequently I spent the entire day hearing what was on their hearts, affirming, and praying with them. Afterward they would express their sincere appreciation for my personal interest in their lives and ministry.

Did I waste my time by not just focusing on promoting the witnessing programs? No! Because witnessing is people, and when we build people up in Christ, we definitely increase the effectiveness of witnessing. Even the secular world recognizes this principle. The Japanese auto makers operating in North America listen to, seek the input of, and take personal interest in their workers and their families. Consequently, their morale, work satisfaction, and production remain quite high. And if such companies, motivated by profit, can apply such Christian principles, why not the church of Christ!

THE SYMPATHIZING CHRIST

Dietrich Bonhoeffer expressed it like this: "The first service that one owes to others . . . consists in listening to them. . . . Many people are looking for an ear that will listen. They do not find it among Christians, because these Christians are talking when they should be listening. . . . Christians have forgotten that the ministry of listening has been committed to them by Him who is Himself the great listener and whose work they would share. We should listen with the ears of God that we may speak the Word of God" (*Life Together,* pp. 97-99).

I am sure many of us have had the experience of having someone profusely thank us for helping him or her with a problem. When we ask how we have helped, we are told that we took time to listen and understand. Often the greatest help we can give, and the greatest help others can receive, is simply to listen to and to value and love one another. Paul Tournier explains that "the people who have helped me the most are not those who have answered my confessions with advice, exhortation or doctrine, but rather those who have listened to me in silence, and then told me of their own personal life, their own difficulties and experiences" (*The Meaning of Persons,* cited in Larson, *Ask Me to Dance,* p. 64).

Keith Miller tells us more specifically how a ministry of listening can profoundly express love and be life-changing. "I think that this basic attention to individuals in the present moment may be the greatest kind of love we can give them. For in a strange way we are giving them our lives in that instant, when we are giving them our whole attention. I have come to believe that this is perhaps the most real way to value a person as a human being—to really be with him and take him seriously as he is. A single such contact may change the whole direction of a life" (*A Second Touch,* pp. 62, 63). However, few people ever experience this sort of listening. To be secure and subdued, focusing with our hearts and minds on what other persons are saying, is not easy. Too often we are distracted while they are talking to us. We may be looking at our watches, other people, or our surroundings—or perhaps we are more polite and subtle than that. Yes, we might be looking at them and pretending to be paying attention, only we are actually biding our time for our turn, or are preoccupied with preparing the answer we are eager to give them. Often we interrupt, trying to continue where we last left off, without attempting to relate it to what the person just said.

This is not really listening. It is rather a competitive sport, a tug-of-war game. As we do it we convey the idea that what we want to say is much more important than what they are saying. In essence we indicate that their words are not worth listening to. Consequently, we give the clear impression they themselves are also not important to us. And how can we convince them that they are important to God if they are not important to us? Such persons leave our presence knowing in their hearts that we do not really care about them—only ourselves.

Wayne McDill considers five vital listening skills on pages 61 and 62 of his book *Making Friends for Christ*. The first one he mentions is "an attitude of genuine interest." We listen because we want to, not because we have to. And we listen not primarily for our sake, but for that of the other person. The second listening skill is "eye contact." Where are our eyes focused when we are trying to listen? Are they absorbed in what is being said, or are they bored and searching for something more interesting?

The third skill is "facial expressions." We might succeed at forcing our eyes to concentrate on the person talking to us, but facial expressions can easily betray where our mind really is. Do they show that we are affected by what we hear? Such expressions can reveal whether we are sympathetic or unfeeling, engaged or distracted. The fourth skill involves being aware of "gestures" such as the movements of the head, hands, and the whole body. Such gestures, even though we may not be conscious of them at the time, nevertheless give subtle clues to the other person and convey a message of their own. Finally, the "responses" we give, such as a laugh, a smile, asking a point of clarification, a nod, etc., demonstrate whether we are directly in the flow of the conversation. We want to make sure that exploring such listening skills does not leave us self-conscious about our every gesture or facial expression. At the same time, however, we must remember that all of these skills offer an honest expression of how we really feel on the inside. What we primarily need to concentrate on is that Christ's love really comes through in our lives, and that we genuinely care about others. If that is indeed the case, then everything else will work out all right.

Then McDill discusses seven "signals and symptoms" that we need to watch for as we sympathetically listen to others. Being alert to such signals and symptoms will reveal a great deal about their attitude and outlook on themselves, others, and life in general. That will help us understand them, and effectively witness to them. It will suffice here to just list them: (1) boredom, (2) attitude toward oneself, (3) complaining and griping, (4) alienation and conflict, (5) guilt, (6) fear and worry, and (7) anger, resentment, and bitterness (pp. 62-64).

While we are on this important subject, we must mention some specific don'ts in listening. We've already hinted at some of them, but Jard DeVille, a Christian professor of psychology, gives quite a helpful list. Under the heading "Mistakes in Listening," he enumerates several cautions:

1. "Prejudging people by assuming what their answers will be."

2. "Spending too much time on facts and not enough on feelings."

3. "Ignoring the real meaning of the words the other person uses."

4. "Letting our feelings block our sensitivity to his needs."

5. "Permitting ourselves to be distracted by our own secular interests."

6. "Pretending to listen while planning to take charge as soon as he pauses for breath."

7. "Going off on tangents which do not lead him toward Christ" (*The Psychology of Witnessing,* pp. 84, 85).

In summary we must always keep fresh in our minds that Christ is the source of all true listening, compassion, empathy, and sympathy. We will do well in these important areas only if we stay in continual communion with Him. Christ, our example and high priest, is not someone "who is unable to sympathize with our weaknesses, but one who in every respect has been tempted as we are'' (Heb. 4:15). And as we experience His sympathy with our weaknesses, we can show the same kind of sympathy toward others.

A pastor related an incident that took place in his church as a disheveled man apparently walked in off the street right in the middle of his sermon. The visitor started looking for an empty seat in the back, but failing to find one, he walked slowly down the aisle searching. And not finding any, he kept on going to the front of the sanctuary. By this time the stranger had produced a lot of commotion among the worshipers. Not finding a seat when he reached the front and not seeing anyone offering him any, he simply squatted down right there in the aisle in front of the entire stunned congregation.

As he sat there listening to the rest of the sermon, an old deacon approached the strange and unexpected visitor. ''What will the deacon do?'' the people wondered. ''Will he usher him out, or will he . . . ?'' To the amazement of everyone present, the old deacon touched his shoulder and squatted down right next to him! This is truly what it means to sympathize.

CHAPTER

SIX

———

CHRIST THE ANSWER TO OUR NEEDS

The New York *Times* printed a United Press release from Rome several years ago about a Mrs. Concetta Brigante who climbed out of a seventh-floor window of her apartment building and balanced on the ledge. The neighbors, naturally frantic, called the police. Firemen put up a ladder and forcibly rescued Mrs. Brigante. Nobody listened to her protests, and she was taken to a mental clinic as a would-be suicide. At the clinic Mrs. Brigante finally got to tell her story. She was housecleaning and accidentally locked herself in her room. She was merely trying to get into the room next door via the ledge'' (Larson, pp. 9, 10).

Larson's amusing yet sad story teaches us two points: First, we really do not often hear what others are really saying. We come to a situation with our minds blocked with preconceived ideas and presuppositions. "I've already made up my mind, so don't confuse me with the facts." Second, consequently, we fail to meet people at their real level of need. In other words, we scratch, but we do not "scratch where it itches." How can we effectively minister to people's needs without first of all becoming acquainted with what they are?

It is like blindly shooting and desperately hoping that one of the bullets might possibly hit the target. I have a friend who explains his witnessing technique by actually saying that he does not need to listen to people because he bombards them with many ideas and programs. One of them will surely somehow work. He is really convinced that listening and sympathizing in order to discover felt needs is just a waste of time.

Even Jesus, the expert witness, took time to listen and sympathize, and then meet people's needs. And following His example not only helps us to understand people and effectively minister to their needs and hurts, but to also win their hearts and trust. Jesus took time to socialize with a sinner and an outcast like Zacchaeus (Luke 19:1-10), and in the process determined and satisfied his needs of understanding and acceptance. He dialogued with the rich young ruler (Mark 10:17-27), continuing to comment on his question even after the man had left sadly. In fact, Jesus' heart went out in compassion for him, for He longed to meet his spiritual need. Scripture states that "Jesus looking upon him loved him" (verse 21).

In such personal contacts, people "came to Christ or met Him in a natural way. The aggressive hard sell was absent. He never seemed to be selling a product to them in an artificial way. His evangelism always seemed to be a natural result of His interest in them as persons, and it was directly related to their needs" (James H. Jauncey, *One-on-One Evangelism,* p. 11).

Some witnessing programs, sad to say, encourage the participants not to listen, not to sympathize and discover human needs. Their proponents claim that such personal involvement distracts the Christian from presenting the meat of the "gospel." A pastor visited a hurting former member to encourage him to go back to church. But whenever the individual tried to share some of his spiritual wounds, the pastor would say, "Brother, this is *chaff* you are talking about. You shouldn't be thinking about that, but about *grain.*" Maybe so, but the person did not return to church because he obviously did not sense that the pastor was really interested in him as a person, how he felt, and his particular needs.

Such methods arm their adherents with a memorized speech. They rush ahead with their canned presentation regardless of

CHRIST THE ANSWER TO OUR NEEDS

what the poor recipient might say. And if by chance he catches them off guard (when they cough, sneeze, or yawn!) with a comment, they nervously wait for him to finish, then quickly pick up where they left off without any consideration to what the person was trying to communicate.

I once had two door to-door witnesses stop by my home. After I invited the clean-cut, sincere young men into my living room, they proceeded immediately to rattle off their memorized program without giving me any chance to interject. Winding down at last, they then invited me to commit myself to the beliefs they had just finished presenting. At last I had my chance to say something. I asked them if they were at all interested in knowing who I was. Was I a converted Christian or not? Did they care to know about any ideas or questions I had? Did they want to find out if I had any particular needs, spiritual or otherwise? Because they were not prepared for any type of interaction, my questions only added to their bewilderment. Finally one of them, wanting to get down to business, abruptly demanded if I wanted to accept their doctrines or not. They were in a hurry to contact other people who might be more receptive.

I do not want to be too hard on them. At least they were doing something. And I can understand how easy it is to get so wrapped up in our programs or points of doctrine that we become unmindful of people, their pains and problems. I will never forget the Bible study I gave to Sam. He seemed quite distracted, continually attempting to divert my attention from my important study. But, vigorously pressing on, I tried to delicately overlook his interruptions.

In my unbalanced commitment to the truth I felt compelled to use my time efficiently, and not let anything divert me from the important task of teaching God's Word. Finding it impossible to hold it in any longer, Sam insisted that he just had to talk to me about something that was weighing heavily on his mind. With an apology he said that he was not able to pay attention to the lesson because his mind was on his wife, who had taken the car and the kids and had left earlier that week.

Two days before, he had arrived home from work to find a note from her stating that she was tired of it all, and that she was leaving him for good. Setting my study aside, I attentively listened to him, ashamed that I had actually put a presentation on the state of the dead above his desperate need for a friend to talk to.

Some may even pretend that they would like to know more about our religion, but inwardly they are really longing for true friendship and belonging. Dr. Jauncey, an expert in personal witnessing, relates his experience with Hugo, a college student who felt quite insignificant and ignored on the campus. Hugo had sought Jauncey out after a meeting to inquire about some biblical questions. However Dr. Jauncey sensed that the young man was not really interested in the answers he gave him. "It was only after I began to ask about him personally that I became aware of the extent of his misery," Jauncey relates. "He did not really need any answers. He needed *me,* someone to relate to, someone to show an interest in him" (*ibid.*, pp. 37, 38).

Unfortunately, not all Christian leaders are of the same caliber as Jauncey in terms of relational witnessing. Sometimes even evangelists and ministers treat living human beings as objects or machines to use, manipulate, and fit into their own scheme of things. Once I attended an evangelistic meeting where the speaker waxed eloquently about God's love, and how we needed to demonstrate it in down-to-earth ways. Deeply impressed by what I had heard, I wanted to thank him and share a spiritual need with him. Even though I had barely started to talk, he abruptly cut me off and pushed me aside. He did not even ask my name. It was quite a rude awakening for me to suddenly realize that he did not really care about individuals in the audience as persons. Because he was just interested in netting as many souls as possible, they meant nothing to him personally. Another deplorable variation is using something as sacred as prayer to hurriedly get rid of someone seeking our help. Such behavior makes a travesty of the gospel of Christ, especially by those who should know better. The gospel must not only proceed from our lips, but must also flow from our lives.

No matter who we are, or what our background is, we all share the same fundamental needs. At the very core of our being each one of us has the universal need to accept and to be accepted, to love and to be loved, to trust and to be trusted, to be free and to be fulfilled. Psychologist Abraham Maslow is well known for his hierarchy of human motives or needs. These basic and universal needs fall into five categories listed in an increasing order of importance. First, the physiological needs. Second, the need for safety. Third, belonging and love. Fourth, self-esteem. And fifth, the drive for self-actualization (see *Motivation and Personality*, pp. 88-106).

Maslow argues that not all needs are dominant at the same moment in human experience. Rather the one that remains unfulfilled becomes the focus of attention, and we do not try to fulfill any higher needs until we have met the lower ones. For example, a person does not seek self-esteem and self-actualization unless he has satisfied his lack of belonging and love.

Jesus was thoroughly acquainted with the basic and pressing human needs as He mingled with people. That is why He, the Bread of Life and the Great Physician, fed the hungry and healed the sick. He did not have to touch the leper in order to heal him. That touch was not necessary for his physical cure, but very essential for his emotional healing. Our Saviour knew that this outcast desperately required acceptance and love. Before He healed him "he stretched out His hand and touched him" (see Mark 1:40-42). Since the Jews ostracized the Samaritans, Jesus knew that the Samaritan woman needed to experience acceptance and respect from Him, a Jew. That is the reason why He, the Water of Life, asked her for a drink of water (see John 4:7-10).

It is imperative to take time to get acquainted with people and see their needs surface. That will keep us from substituting prepackaged programs for needed sympathy and love. In fact it is often better not to help than to offer them irrelevant assistance. For instance, treating someone with a severe headache by putting medicated cream on his toe instead of giving him Tylenol for his actual pain will only leave him even worse off.

One hot and muggy Sunday I was seeding my lawn and covering it with sawdust. By the end of the day I was quite tired, filthy, and itching all over. Needing immediate relief before taking a bath, I asked my wife to scratch a particularly itchy place right in the middle of my back, one that had proved quite elusive. Not knowing precisely where the spot was, she dutifully groped for it. Getting frustrated after a few failed attempts, I guided her hand to the irritating spot, and what a relief when she finally found it.

Do we sometimes reach out to people in such a haphazard way that we do not touch them where they hurt? For Christ, people and their needs came first. And they clearly sensed that He understood what they were experiencing. He was there to meet them at the level of their need.

Now we must consider what we may refer to as the reciprocity, or the give-and-take, in ministering to human needs. When we reach out to others, do we find ourselves always in the giving position and them in the receiving? But people will more readily accept our help if they know that they too can assist us in some way. Not many people like to always be on the receiving end. They want to feel that others need them in some way.

I can honestly say that I do not recall ever meeting a person I did not learn something from. In fact, one can accumulate a lot of interesting and practical knowledge from just taking an interest in what others think and do. At the same time we may win their trust by letting them know that they too can help us. Because we also, like them, have our own questions and needs, we need to not only be helpers, but "helpees" as well.

After I had given a chapel talk on reciprocity at a grade school, I met Danny, a student whom I had helped solve a problem earlier that week. After again expressing his great appreciation for my assistance, he stated that he wanted to reciprocate by doing something for me. "I'd like to buy you lunch at that restaurant across the street," he hesitantly started. "Would you go there with me?"

"Danny, come on now. Don't worry about it," I replied. "I was just glad to help you." But when he continued to press me to go, I acquiesced, reminding myself that I needed to practice what I had been preaching. I could sense his delight that he was able to do something nice for someone else.

Carl Kromminga argues that allowing the ones we reach out to to help us in some way often gives them a sense of self-worth as well as the added insight or incentive to become less self-centered. "The Christian, too, has needs. There are times when he can call on the neighbor for help and assistance. The appeal will give the neighbor a sense of his value and worth in the relationship. Perhaps when he has an opportunity to help as well as be helped, he will begin to be liberated from the grip of self-concern and self-interest" (*Bringing God's News to Neighbors,* p. 141).

Jesus, as our great example in witnessing, willingly ate dinner at Zacchaeus' house. Even though it was really the tax collector who needed help, Jesus provided him with an opportunity to serve and show Him kindness (see Luke 19:1-10). And even though He aided Lazarus and his sisters Mary and Martha in many ways, He frequently accepted and appreciated their gracious hospitality (see Luke 10:38-42). Ellen White tells us that "at the home of Lazarus, Jesus had often found rest. The Saviour had no home of His own; He was dependent on the hospitality of His friends and disciples. . . . He longed for human tenderness, courtesy, and affection" (*The Desire of Ages,* p. 524).

He asked the Samaritan woman to offer Him water to drink, knowing that He was to give her the Water of Life (see John 4). Even though He was a Jew, "He accepted the hospitality of this despised people [the Samaritans]. He slept with them under their roofs, ate with them at their tables" (*The Ministry of Healing,* p. 26). Moreover, He, the Bread of Life, who could have created great quantities of bread out of nothing, was willing to use the donation of the lad with the five loaves and two fishes (see John 6:8-14).

And in the Garden of Gethsemane He hoped His three disciples would stay awake and pray for Him (see Matt. 26:36-46). "The human heart longs for sympathy in suffering. This longing Christ felt to the very depths of His being. In the supreme agony of His soul He came to His disciples with a yearning desire to hear some words of comfort from those whom He had so often blessed and comforted" (*The Desire of Ages,* p. 687).

Harry Williams writes about a woman who met a Christian who talked with her about her need to be saved and to attend the church while at the same time totally ignoring an obvious need—her broken arm. She said: "He talked to me an hour about my soul and his church but never once asked what was wrong with my arm." Then Williams deduces two important points: First, "we may not be able to touch one where he is really hurting without first touching where he thinks he hurts most." Second, when we touch a person where he thinks he hurts the most, we must also keep in mind that there might very well be a much more urgent need ("Prime Time People," in James A. Ponder, ed., *Motivating Laymen to Witness,* pp. 79, 80).

We live in a complex world full of people going through terrible ordeals and difficulties. Sometimes they are so confused that they just do not know what their real needs are. As they grope for answers, they require our patient and sympathetic guidance. Of course, we must pay attention to the broken arm first, but we must also be aware of the bruised heart. Love cannot just allow us to be so preoccupied with meeting external needs that we neglect to discern inward ones.

Let us suppose that we are conducting a dietary program for the prevention of heart disease. If we truly love the individuals who attend it, would we be merely interested in improving their nutrition so that they might not die of a heart attack, yet ignore the far more serious problem of spiritual and eternal death because of a corrupt heart? Genuine love directs us to see the perceived needs, yet it also propels us to discern the deep-rooted needs of the soul. And when we show genuine interest in people's visible needs, they often—to their own surprise—reveal their invisible ones.

The Gospels show Jesus' skill in balancing both the apparent and hidden needs in ministering to others. For example, He was interested not only in physical thirst, but also in spiritual craving. He did not care just about physical eyesight, but also spiritual insight. When He healed bodily leprosy, He also dealt with the leprosy of sin. Besides identifying with people, He also sought their transformation. Following Christ's example will motivate us, for example, to conduct all our health programs not as an end in themselves, but as a bridge leading us to meet the needs of spiritual health. I remember the occasions when I conducted different community health programs. The church members helping me would pray for the participants, befriending them, talking and listening to them, sitting next to them, and seeing them off to the parking lot at the end of each evening.

It was always gratifying to see what transpired. Meaningful relationships developed between the members and those attending. And it was natural at the end of the week to hear such comments as "We sure hope this will not be the last time we'll see you," "Let's remember to keep in touch," or "If you happen to be in the area where we live, please feel free to drop by." Such friendships would lead us to minister to their spiritual needs as well.

Now we must address some practical aspects of ministering to people's diverse needs. For example, we must always keep in mind that while we can do our part, we cannot solve all the world's problems. Only Christ can. And as members of His body, given various spiritual gifts and governed by Him as the head, we must let Him work through us.

The experience of Peter and John as they healed the lame man on their way to worship at the Temple reveals some important principles in dealing with human needs. When the cripple asked him and John for money at the Temple gate, Peter replied, "I have no silver and gold, but I give you what I have; in the name of Jesus Christ of Nazareth, walk" (Acts 3:6). His words suggest the following insights: First, people rarely see beyond their present predicament. Nor are they always aware that it is their real needs that really hurt the most. Perhaps they have ceased to hope that there actually exists real help for their real problems. We can understand then why they become engrossed in satisfying their superficial lacks.

Second, such individuals often cannot imagine ahead of time whether or how we can meet their deeper needs, but when we do, they respond with intense gratitude. Harry Williams wonders what the healed man would have done if he had been asked whether he preferred money or a restored body. Williams suggests that "he would have said, 'Give me strong legs and feet and I won't have to beg alms again. Yes, by all means help me to walk!' " (in Ponder, p. 80). Then Williams answers the question he raises as to why the lame man did not ask for healing in the first place. "He didn't understand his options. He simply did not know that being able to walk again was a possibility" (*ibid.*). Williams goes on to admonish us that "if we are merely tossing coins to the multitudes, we may well be giving the world what it is requesting but failing to give it what it really needs" (*ibid.*). Then he clarifies that while Christian social ministries are vital, they must not be an end in themselves—rather they must lead us to be involved in a deeper spiritual ministry. "But a church fails the world," he further explains, "when it spends all its time and resources distributing alms and never gets around to saying to the crippled in sin: 'In the name of Jesus rise up and walk!'. . . We need to touch people but must take care that we touch them as Jesus did: where they are hurting and when they are hurting but especially where and when they are hurting the most" (*ibid.*, p. 81).

Third, when it comes to meeting people's diverse needs, we can only give what we have. Peter and John could not offer what they did not possess—silver and gold—but what they did have—the healing of Christ. In a world bursting at the seams with complex human needs and problems, we must take stock of our strengths and weaknesses, of what we can do for others and what we cannot. Each one of us has different talents and spiritual gifts for the equipment of the saints "for the work of ministry, for building up the body of Christ" (Eph. 4:12). For further study of the different types of spiritual gifts, see Romans 12, 1 Corinthians 12, and Ephesians 4.

And the various gifts, under the headship of Christ, complement each other, so that if we cannot meet some particular needs, other members of the body might be able to. As followers of Christ, none of us has all the gifts of the Spirit, but we all must have all the fruits of the Spirit such as "love, joy, peace, patience, kindness" (Gal. 5:22, 23). That is why, even though we might not be able to give others complete help, we can show them love and kindness, and we can direct them to other members of the body who may be qualified in the area of their specific need.

Therefore, even though we cannot do all that must be done, we can at least try to find help, sympathize, and show that we truly care. "During World War I a soldier was mortally wounded in no-man's-land between the two lines of trenches. He called for his friend to come and help him. The friend turned to his officer and said, 'Sir, give me permission to go bring him back.' The officer said, 'No! He will be dead by the time you get there.' But the friend persisted.

"Finally the officer relented and said, 'All right, go ahead.' The soldier climbed out of the trench. He was hit by enemy fire. After a period of time he came crawling back toward the trench dragging the body of his buddy. The officer said, 'What did I tell you? He is dead! And you are wounded! What did you accomplish?' The soldier replied, 'Sir, he was not dead when I got there. When he saw me, he said, "You know, I knew you would come" ' " (Delos Miles, *Overcoming Barriers to Witnessing,* p. 67).

When we take interest in people and endeavor to meet their needs, we must ask ourselves, As we commune with others, are we communing with Christ? Are we listening to His voice, allowing Him to guide us in every way? While trying to satisfy the needs of others, do we at the same time allow Him to meet our own? Are we anchored securely and strongly in Him? Yes, we must reach out and minister to others, but we must do so from a position of strength in Christ, and not from one of personal weakness. Only Christ alone is sufficient for the great challenges of helping with the diverse and difficult needs all around us!

Finally, I want to share a clever fairy tale by Wes Seeliger.

"Once upon a time there was a frog. But he really wasn't a frog. He was a prince who looked and felt like a frog. A wicked witch had cast a spell on him. Only the kiss of a beautiful maiden could save him. But since when do cute chicks kiss frogs? So there he sat, unkissed prince in frog form. But miracles happen. One day a beautiful maiden grabbed him up and gave him a big smack. *Crash! Boom! Zap!* There he was, a handsome prince. And you know the rest. They lived happily ever after. So what is the task of the Church? To kiss frogs, of course" (in *Faith at Work* [1972], p. 13).

I once presented this story at a youth meeting to encourage the young people to affirm and love others around them, and then watch their miraculous transformation into princes of Christ. Later on that day I met two young women in the library who were giggling nervously while pointing to a magazine in their hands. Curious about what might be so funny, I insisted on seeing it. Stalling, they kept laughing and saying, "You won't believe it! It is so funny!" Finally, they showed me a set of four cartoons. The first revealed an ugly and miserable frog, all alone. The second portrayed a beautiful princess approaching the ugly frog. The third had the princess holding and kissing it. "So far nothing unusual or funny," I commented.

"Just wait!" they urged. When they showed me the fourth cartoon, it did not reveal, as one would expect, a handsome prince and a beautiful princess living happily ever after, but rather two ugly frogs!

Seeliger asserts that the church's task is to kiss frogs. That is figuratively true, but we must also add that before we do that we must be "kissed" by the Prince of Life. Only then can we transform them into His princes and princesses.

CHAPTER

SEVEN

CHRIST CAN BE TRUSTED

Leaving Seattle and heading toward Portland on Interstate 5, I could clearly see in the distance thick, dark clouds of ash billowing miles high into the blue Washington sky. Earlier that fateful Sunday morning of late May 1980, Mount St. Helens had rumbled and violently exploded, spewing out more than 1.5 cubic miles of debris. The tremendous volcanic blast had a force estimated at about 500 times that of the bomb dropped on Hiroshima.

At the time of the explosion David Crockett of Seattle's KOMO-TV was standing at the base of the mountain, trapped. Desperately trying to keep from being buried alive, Crockett bravely kept moving and speaking into his recorder. "I am walking toward the only light I can see. I can hear the mountain rumble. At this very moment I have to say, 'Honest to God, I believe I am dead.' The ash in my eyes burns my eyes, burns my eyes! Oh dear God, this is hell! It's very, very hard to breathe and very dark. If I could only breathe air. God, just give me a breath! . . . Ash is coming down on me heavily. It's either dark or I am dead. God, I want to live!" ("God, I Want to Live!" *Time*, June 2, 1980, p. 26).

David Crockett survived, rescued by helicopter, but a number of people were not so lucky. Searchers found their bodies later. One of the victims was Harry Truman, a gruff and rugged old man who lived in a cabin near the mountain. Harry doggedly refused to be evacuated, asserting on national television that he had lived with Mount St. Helens for 50 long years, that she had been good to him all that time, and that he wouldn't leave because he trusted her. Looking defiantly at the volcano, he said, "No one knows more about this mountain than Harry, and it don't dare blow up on him." The eruption buried him and his cabin (*ibid.*).

We may say that the mountain betrayed his trust. The untrustworthiness of Mount St. Helens can symbolize the uncertainty pervading our world. People, things, and circumstances —they all change. And when we think our mountain is invincible and unshakable, we are just setting up ourselves for disappointment.

The only mountain that is perfectly solid and unshakable is Mount Zion, the biblical symbol of the Lord and those who put their ultimate confidence in Him. "Those who trust in the Lord are like Mount Zion which cannot be moved, but abides for ever" (Ps. 125:1). While we live in the midst of distrust, uncertainty, and changeableness, in Christ we have a friend who is perfectly trustworthy and reliable, and "the same yesterday and today and for ever" (Heb. 13:8). And only as we draw trust from Him, the source, can we gain people's confidence so as to lead them to Him.

We may not be as stubborn as Harry Truman, but we all have an innate need to trust someone. The basic need to trust and to be trusted goes hand in hand with that to love and be loved, and is as necessary to life as the air that photographer Crockett fought for. On the other hand, distrust and suspicion suffocate just as surely as did the gray ash filling his lungs. A trusting relationship is one of the highest spheres of human existence, for where there is trust there is love and life. And in having Christ's love and life, we become more like Him. "When men will show confidence in their fellowmen they will come much nearer to possessing the mind of Christ" (*Testimonies to Ministers,* p. 189).

Thus to trust and to be trusted is to have the mind of Christ. And to have the mind of Christ reflected in our lives is to be loving, sympathetic, and of one accord. We will do nothing from selfishness or conceit, will seek to be humble and to count others as better than ourselves, and will look out for their interests (Phil. 2:1-8). Jesus won people's confidence. The fourth step of Christ's method—His gaining of their trust and confidence—resulted from His mingling with them as one desiring their good, listening and sympathizing with them, and ministering to their needs (see *The Ministry of Healing,* p. 143).

Since Lucifer distrusted God in heaven, suspicion has infected all creation. Nations and peoples are wary of each other. We cannot find a single place in society immune to distrust—including, unfortunately, the family. Infidelity, for example, has broken down confidence between husbands and wives. And if people cannot even have trust in the closest of human relationships, then all society is in real trouble. "Men and women who this week declare their undying allegiance to each other next week are walking out on each other" (Keller, *Salt for Society,* p. 134). Indeed we can trace all damaged human relationships and social problems back to distrust.

That does not mean that people do not have their own valid reasons for being distrustful. Many have been exploited, manipulated, and otherwise taken advantage of. Perhaps they found themselves caught in a crooked business transaction, or maybe they tried to be good Samaritans and got burned. As a result they erect a shield around themselves and announce that never again will they allow themselves to be hurt again. "We've learned our lesson," they defensively assert. "Enough is enough."

One scorching summer day some years ago I tried to sell my well-maintained two-door sedan. I had put an ad in the newspaper, washed and waxed the car, and parked it right on the front lawn of my corner-lot house. Shortly afterward I received a call from an elderly woman who wanted to bring her friend along to see the car. Anticipating their arrival, I felt good that the ad had paid off so quickly. When I answered the door, I saw two apprehensive-looking women.

As we headed toward the car, their questions showed how suspicious they were. "You don't really change the oil, do you?" they asked. "Is that the real mileage on the odometer? It sure looks like it has been in a bad accident." I remember trying to hide my annoyance while attempting to defend my good vehicle (and also myself). Then they wanted to take it for a ride. After letting me get into the back seat, they slid onto the front and headed down the street.

As they drove aimlessly around town, I tried to remain calm as they kept peppering me with more questions. Finally one got to me. We were then in the middle of a heat wave, and I was cooped up in the back seat, perspiring profusely (the car had no air conditioner). "Does the heater work?" they demanded.

"Why wouldn't it?" I responded impatiently. "Car heaters always work, don't they! Come on, ladies, why talk about heaters now, especially in this kind of weather?"

Just then they actually turned the heater on! The car was getting unbearably hot, and to my horror a cloud of vapor and smoke poured from the heat vents, filling the car. It seemed incredible to me that there could possibly be anything wrong with the heater, but I am sure that the smoke convinced them that I was trying to sell them a lemon after all. Coughing and bewildered, they spotted a house on a corner lot that looked to them like mine. Driving straight onto the stranger's front lawn, they flung the doors open and fled. And that was the last I saw of them.

I struggled out of the back seat only to confront a puzzled, furious, and suspicious man who was wondering what in the world was going on, and why I had parked on his recently watered lawn. What could I say? I promptly apologized, trying to explain. But I knew that the best thing I could do under the circumstances was to leave quickly.

Can we really blame people for becoming more and more distrusting of almost everyone and everything? Look at what has happened to the American savings and loan industry. It was supposed to be the most conservative and safe type of investment for the average American family. But because of the greed and corruption of some officials, the taxpayers will have to pour literally billions of dollars into its rescue. We have always heard that you really cannot trust politicians and lawyers, but now even evangelists and ministers have come under a cloud of suspicion after the well-publicized scandals that have rocked the church and the country.

Where do people then turn to find trust? How are we, Christ's disciples, going to win their confidence? And if we cannot, then who can fill that void?

We will not find answers in what this world has to offer, because genuine love and trustworthiness come only from God, its source. He did not wait for human beings to become trustworthy before entrusting them with His only Son. The all-trustworthy God trusted the totally untrustworthy in order to draw them close to Himself, transform, and redeem them. All because of His great love for us. "He [Christ] honored man with His confidence, and thus placed him on his honor" (*Testimonies to Ministers*, p. 190).

It is crucial that we win people's trust and confidence as we lead them to Christ. And the only way to accomplish that is through Christ living in us and ministering through us. The following principles will help us to model our attempts to win trust after His divine approach:

1. When we reach out to others, they definitely need to sense that we have their best interest at heart—that we are not manipulating them for some ulterior motive but have genuine concern for them for their own sake. For the great value that God has already invested in each one of them. Like Jesus, we need to reach "the hearts of the people by going among them as one who desired their good" (*The Desire of Ages,* p. 151).

2. They must know for sure that we will remain friends even if they do not attend our church or get baptized. It is just not consistent with Christ's love to be friendly to others when we need them for whatever motive, and then all of a sudden dump them simply because we have no use for them anymore. This sadly happens all too often. "Unfortunately, many non-Christians today are suspicious of all Christians because of a previous contact with a friendly religious person who had ulterior motives. Some non-Christians refuse to listen to a single word about our Lord until they're sure we'll be their friends regardless. . . . We must love each person for himself" (Little, *How to Give Away Your Faith,* p. 52).

3. As true Christians we must listen to them, identify and sympathize with them. Christ's "strong personal sympathy helped to win hearts" (*The Desire of Ages,* p. 151). Moreover, "by visiting the people, talking, praying, sympathizing with them, you will win hearts." Ellen White describes this "as the highest missionary work" that we can do (*Testimonies to the Church,* vol. 9, p. 41).

4. We must do all we can to minister to their needs as we gradually become aware of them. First we must remember that often people simply want to be accepted, want to have a friend, want to be included in our activities. Ralph Neighbour was right on target when he said, "It's hard for people to really believe we want them in heaven if we don't want them in our living room" (*Witness, Take the Stand,* p. 42).

5. Using little acts of kindness, words of encouragement, a genuine handshake, we must prepare a path to their hearts. Such simple things win trust, not because they involve a lot of time or effort, but rather because of the genuine spirit in which we do them. Even the way we shake someone's hand can carry great significance. "Much depends upon the manner in which you meet those whom you visit. You can take hold of a person's hand in greeting in such a way as to gain his confidence at once, or in so cold a manner that he will think you have no interest in him" (*Gospel Workers,* p. 189).

Also asking a simple favor of someone, letting him know we need him and are willing to accept his kindness, can contribute to building trust. Jesus demonstrated this fact when He asked the Samaritan woman for a drink of water. That simple act helped to break down barriers that had accumulated for years, and showed her that Jesus accepted and trusted her. Tradition said that Samaritan women were always ceremonially unclean, so devout Jewish men would never accept anything that they had touched. It probably stunned the woman at the well when Jesus accepted water despite the fact that tradition said her very presence had made the vessel that contained it "unclean." But His trust stirred up trust in her own heart. He "was seeking to find the key to this heart, and with the tact born of divine love, He asked, not offered, a favor. The offer of a kindness might have been rejected; but trust awakens trust. The King of heaven came to this outcast soul, asking a service at her hands. . . . [He] was dependent upon a stranger's kindness for even the gift of a drink of water'' (*The Desire of Ages*, p. 184).

6. Just as much as "trust awakens trust," so also distrust produces distrust. If we act apprehensive and suspicious toward others, we will trigger similar feelings toward us. People will likely become cautious and conclude that there must be some reason for our wary behavior. On the other hand, if we come across as amiable, reassuring, and reasonably trusting, they will likely respond in kind, a principle I repeatedly saw in operation as a missionary traveling to different countries in Africa. For instance, when dealing with different government officials at airports, I observed that these total strangers often become much more relaxed and trusting if I approached them with an open, confident attitude.

Certainly Zacchaeus had no reputation for trustworthiness. On the contrary, he was notorious for his fraudulent tax-collecting practices. But when Jesus showed him acceptance and trust in going to his home, it awakened his nobler characteristics, and he yearned to prove himself worthy of Christ's friendship and trust. One cannot help getting the impression that the publican was just biding his time till someone like Jesus would believe and show confidence in him. People had constantly looked down on him, making it difficult for him to extricate himself from his predicament. But Jesus freed him.

Ellen White movingly describes how Jesus inspired and won the confidence of those coming in contact with Him. She writes, "In every human being He discerned infinite possibilities. . . . Looking upon them with hope, He inspired hope. Meeting them with confidence, He inspired trust. . . . In His presence souls despised and fallen realized that they still were men, and they longed to prove themselves worthy of His regard. In many a heart that seemed dead to all things holy, were awakened new impulses. To many a despairing one there opened the possibility of a new life'' (*Education*, p. 80).

7. We must say what we mean, and mean what we say. Furthermore, we must not only teach the truth, but be truthful

CHRIST'S WAY OF REACHING PEOPLE

people, telling truthful things. Doing so will always win confidence. As Christians we must be men and women of our word, for otherwise we lose our credibility. "A man may not bear the most pleasant exterior, he may be deficient in many respects; but if he has a reputation for straightforward honesty, he will gain the confidence of others" (*Testimonies,* vol. 4, p. 353).

A certain pastor would accept appointments to meet with people in his office, but frequently would not keep them. It did not take long for people to learn that he was not dependable. Certainly, being unreliable does not help us to gain trust. "Dishonesty is practiced all through our ranks. . . . I am pained to make the statement that there is an alarming lack of honesty even among Sabbathkeepers" (*ibid.,* p. 310). "Everything that Christians do should be as transparent as the sunlight. Truth is of God; deception, in every one of its myriad forms, is of Satan" (*Thoughts From the Mount of Blessing,* p. 68).

Keller comments on how shameless dishonesty fills our sophisticated, yet artificial, society. "Our culture conditions us to live behind a false facade of geniality. We are sophisticated to the point where we can pretend to be other than we are. Our civilized cynicism leads many 'to smile in your face while slitting your jugular vein' " (p. 133).

8. To represent Christ properly, we must never betray sacred trust. Sometimes we divulge and misrepresent personal things shared with us in confidence. Keeping confidence helps us to win confidence, but breaking it causes us to lose it.

9. Above all, we need to practice what we preach and teach. People will respond with trust when they see that our lives are consistent with our words. Jesus won confidence because His life demonstrated what He taught.

Keller explains that to be the spiritual salt in people's lives is to be reliable, loyal, and trustworthy. An ancient and widespread tradition uses salt to affirm loyal and trusting relationships between people. Commenting on society's desperate need for such relationships, he states that people exclaim when he does what he says he would. "This simple straightforward, solid reliability in the daily deportment of a Christian will do more to foster and generate fidelity in others than all the preaching of a lifetime. Not only will it encourage our contemporaries to put confidence in us, but much more importantly it will lead them, eventually, to meet the Master and put their trust in Him'' (*ibid.*, pp. 134, 135).

It is not difficult to trust the trustworthy, but we may wonder sometimes if we should trust—or how to trust—some individuals whose integrity we question. Perhaps we should avoid them and have nothing to do with them. What if we risk trusting persons in whom our trust does not awaken theirs in response? What then? Doesn't trusting dubious people in an idealistic fashion make us too vulnerable and reveal us as naive and impractical?

Of course, we take a risk anytime we show genuine love and trust. But that does not mean that we have to do it with our eyes closed. Like Jesus, we show trust in others while knowing full well what the problems and potential risks are. The prophets and Jesus and His disciples demonstrated clearly in their suffering and death that love is a dangerous business. But just as Christ's love compelled Him to take chances, so also His love flowing in our lives leads us to do the same.

Here are some considerations and suggestions that may help us in knowing why we should and how to caringly yet wisely take risks in trusting others:

1. Jesus trusts us when we are not trustworthy because He loves us and desires to inspire reciprocal hope and trust in us. While we are by no means worthy of His trust, He gives us it anyway. Should not we reflect the same attitude as we relate to others?

2. If we follow Christ's method of mingling, listening, and sympathizing, we will become acquainted with the other person and his particular needs, and as a consequence approach the situation in a more effective way.

3. We must recognize that it is impossible to always determine a person's trustworthiness. Sometimes we will be surprised about people. Those we least expect to be trustworthy may display it, while those we put great confidence in may disappoint us.

4. When we risk trusting others, we must remember that we are not alone. Christ is right there with us, experiencing the

consequences with us. Some of the people whom He helped, loved, and trusted turned against Him. Thus Jesus not only understands our challenges, but He promised to give us everything necessary to accomplish His work through us.

5. Even though the act of trusting people may not awaken trust in each one of them—it is their choice alone to make—still it does provide the greatest possible incentive for them to respond positively to us. Remember how as children when our parents or teachers expressed confidence in us, we longed to prove ourselves to them?

Henry Stimson, the American statesman who served under five presidents and understood human nature well, once said, "The chief lesson I have learned in a long life is that the only way to make a man trustworthy is to trust him; and the surest way to make him untrustworthy is to distrust him, and show your distrust" ("The Bomb and the Opportunity," *Harper's Magazine,* March 1946).

6. Finally, we need to carefully consider the practical principles in Christ's counsel to His disciples when He commissioned them to go and witness: "Behold, I send you out as sheep in the midst of wolves; so be wise as serpents and innocent as doves" (Matt. 10:16).

a. We do not need to abandon our idealism of showing trust in people. Christ compares us to two harmless and innocent creatures, the sheep and the dove.

b. However, while we need to maintain our idealism, we also need to balance that with practical reality. Christ said that wolves roam out there (and sometimes in sheep's clothing).

c. Jesus asks us to witness in the real world full of sin and sinners. But as we go there, He expects us to keep our eyes wide open. He wants us to be discerning, prudent, and as wise as serpents.

d. Interestingly Christ used a serpent, symbol of Satan, as an object lesson to teach us wisdom. Obviously it is not sufficient to just have the characteristics of a dove in our mixed-up world, but we must also have an important trait of a serpent. While Christ desires us to love, He wants us to love intelligently. And while we must be innocent, He wants wisdom to temper it.

e. Maintaining an essential balance between idealism and pragmatism will prevent us from becoming too apprehensive, or—worse yet—cynical, when it comes to trusting or winning the trust of others. As Stimson said, "the only deadly sin I know is cynicism." The Lord will keep us from turning cynical, losing heart, or becoming weary of doing good works (see Gal. 6:9). Because we love Him, we love others. And in loving and trusting them, we do it as unto the Lord Himself. He opens wide His heart to give us trust, confidence, love, and wisdom.

Of course, ultimate trust resides only in Christ. But when others put their trust in us because they witness His character reflected in the way we relate to them, then it should sway them to accompany us to the Master where together we will put our trust in Him and follow Him. And we must be determined to help them make that crucial connection and transition from us to Christ.

They need to know that we must place ultimate trust in a perfect, unchangeable God, and not in unstable human beings. If we do not direct them to Christ, we are setting them up for disappointment. "We are prone to look to our fellow men for sympathy and uplifting, instead of looking to Jesus. In His mercy and faithfulness God often permits those in whom we place confidence to fail us, in order that we may learn the folly of trusting in man and making flesh our arm. Let us trust fully, humbly, unselfishly in God" (*The Ministry of Healing,* p. 486). And "we need to have far less confidence in what man can do and far more confidence in what God can do for every believing soul" (*Christ's Object Lessons,* p. 146).

That does not mean that they should have no confidence in us at all, or focus it only in Christ. It is not an either/or situation, but rather it is a need to find a proper balance between the two. People naturally place their trust in a person they can see and touch, while it is more difficult to relate to an invisible God. That is why we must be careful here, especially when their trust in us replaces the role of Christ. In putting their trust in us, they must realize that we are only human, with human weaknesses and shortcomings, and that their confidence in us can never be all-sufficient or ultimate. All of us need to trust a perfect

God—perfectly loving, perfectly understanding, perfectly reliable, and perfectly uncapricious. They must also understand that when they find trustworthiness in us, it is not our own doing, but God gave it to us, and He—the source of all good gifts—will bestow it on them, too.

"There stand registered long, hard battles with trying circumstances, perhaps troubles in the home life, that day by day weaken courage, confidence, and faith. Those who are fighting the battle of life at great odds may be strengthened and encouraged by little attentions that cost only a loving effort. To such the strong, helpful grasp of the hand by a true friend is worth more than gold or silver. Words of kindness are as welcome as the smile of angels" (*The Ministry of Healing,* p. 158).

Joan, a church member trying to witness to her colleagues at work, once told me about her reluctance to speak of Christ to those in her office. She said that it was especially difficult for her to reach out to one particular woman. "She smokes too much, she drinks, she is brash," Joan explained. "And furthermore she is so unscrupulous, and her language is something else." When I asked why she was telling me all this, she explained that while she felt it was her Christian duty to witness to her, she just could not force herself to do it. She just could not imagine opening up herself and befriending her. "I am wary of her, and I don't want to get entangled with her problems," she confessed. "Anyway, she is probably not interested in spiritual things."

Joan had to admit, however, that she sensed that God was opening an opportunity to reach the woman. Consequently, guilt troubled her when she found herself avoiding her coworker. Then in her frustration she blurted, "I really cannot help it! I just don't feel comfortable being around her—and frankly, I want nothing to do with her." Quickly adding, "I guess I don't feel I can really trust her," she wondered how God could ever use her to witness when she has such a negative attitude. "I'd do more harm than good."

Finally I asked Joan to tell me, then, why the whole thing was still bothering her. She confessed that when she prayed, the Lord seemed to be impressing her to reach out to the woman. After praying and sympathizing with her, I kindly told her that she should not be looking so much at her colleague and all the possible complications she might have, but rather at Jesus and what He could do through her. I stressed the fact that she had only to start in a small way—a smile, a gesture, a question—see what happened, and then take it from there.

Also I emphasized that what Jesus needed the most in that situation was her availability and not so much her ability. "He can take care of the ability, because He is all-able," I explained, "but He needs us to be available in order for Him to show His ability through us." She readily admitted that she was becoming too worried about herself and what she could or could not do, and overlooking what Christ would do.

A few days later Joan excitedly called to tell me what had transpired at the office with her friend. Notice that this time she described the woman as her "friend." She recounted that later in the week after we had talked, she had asked Christ to help her at the office in spite of herself. When she reached work the next morning, she came face to face with her colleague. Joan said that she strongly felt that God must have providentially arranged that encounter, since all she had to do was to ask a simple question, then mostly listen and sympathize. It seemed that the woman was just waiting for someone who would manifest some genuine caring.

During the conversation the coworker confided that she was worried about her father, who had barely survived a severe heart attack. Also she was quite concerned about her troubled teenage son, who had recently run away from home. Sensing that the woman needed a friend to talk to, Joan stated, "I want you to know that my family and I will be praying for your father and your son every morning."

Astonished at the gesture, the woman's eyes filled with tears as she said, "Thank you! And please don't forget to pray. I need that so much." Then she added, "I tell you, this is the first time anyone ever offered to pray for me. This means a lot, especially now."

As Joan's experience continued to unfold, she said that she had to keep reminding herself that this newly found friend was actually the same "disgusting" woman she had previously dreaded meeting so much. Somehow as Joan focused on what Christ could and would do through her, the heavy burden lifted. And as she became involved in sharing her concern, love, and trust, her heart went out in compassion. The woman now ceased to be an object of disgust and, through Christ, became a focus of sympathy and love. As the weeks passed, their relationship grew. Joan won her trust and confidence, and a few months later she led her to follow Christ and to put her full trust in Him.

Wayne McDill, in summing up what relational evangelism is all about, writes, "They will hear our testimony and look closely to see whether it rings true in our lives. They will come to see Jesus Christ as a trustworthy friend when they find in you and me that same kind of friendship. Then we will have the joy of introducing them to the friend who has laid down His life for them. This is relational evangelism, making friends for Christ" (*Making Friends for Christ,* p. 86).

FOLLOW ME

M ost of us fondly recall the pets we had as children. One of my favorites was a snow-white curly lamb. I remember becoming attached to him at his birth, and in time we became. inseparable friends. He would follow me anywhere at the drop of a hat. You see, he was mine. Whenever he heard me walking, whistling, or calling him, he'd immediately follow. Sometimes I would be quite surprised to discover him trailing right behind me, even though I hadn't done anything to get his attention. It was amazing the way he seemed to sense every move I made. Completely trusting, he would be ready to go wherever I went and do whatever I wanted.

In this chapter we will focus on the fifth step of Christ's method of witnessing. He invited people to follow Him, and they responded eagerly. You see, here was a Man who mingled and identified with them, who knew them by name, and who attentively listened to and keenly sympathized with their varied circumstances. His profound love found a path to their hearts, capturing their confidence. Because He genuinely cared about them, He gave them meaning for the present and hope for the future.

"Had it not been for the sweet, sympathetic spirit that shone out in every look and word, He would not have attracted the large congregations that He did. The afflicted ones who came to Him felt that He linked His interest with theirs as a faithful and tender friend, and they desired to know more of the truths He taught. Heaven was brought near. They longed to abide in His presence, that the comfort of His love might be with them continually" (*The Desire of Ages,* pp. 254, 255).

In John 10:27, one of the several times that Jesus used the expression "follow Me," He describes His relationship to those who responded to Him by saying, "My sheep hear my voice, and I know them, and they follow me." Notice that a personal relationship precedes following Christ. He calls them *"my* sheep." Christ knows them, and they hear and obey His voice. The relationship definitely runs in both directions. Following Christ also implies that they implicitly trust in Him and His leading. The genuine love and interest that the Shepherd shows toward them cannot help drawing them to Him.

John 10:4 states that when Christ, the Good Shepherd, "has brought out all his own, he goes before them, and the sheep follow him, for they know his voice." To be a follower requires a leader who knows and shows the way, for He "goes before them." Sometimes in trying to serve Jesus, we rush ahead of Him, or we get in the way. But to follow Christ is not something mechanical. Rather it is a vital experience that results from a trusting relationship. To follow means to be guided by, to model after, to obey.

Therefore, as Jesus invited people to follow Him during His day, so also we bid them to do the same today. Since we have already won their confidence, they will grasp our hand in trust as we introduce them to our Saviour and Lord. There we will place our hands and theirs in His loving and strong ones, where "no one shall snatch them out" (verse 28). We serve as liaisons connecting them with Christ, while showing them that we also need Him as much as they do. "There are souls perplexed with doubt, burdened with infirmities, weak in faith, and unable to grasp the Unseen, but a friend whom they can see, coming to them in Christ's stead, can be a connecting link to fasten their trembling faith upon Christ" (*ibid.*, p. 297).

In leading lost sheep to the Good Shepherd, we should never think that this important task rests solely on our shoulders.

Instead, we must always remember that Christ intimately involves Himself in rescuing even one lost sheep. He has always been there preparing the way for us to do His work in behalf of the lost. Christ knows their names, and where they live—having even "at times given directions to His servants to go to a certain street in a certain city, to such a house, to find one of His sheep" (*ibid.*, p. 479).

How do we invite them to follow Christ? First of all, the solid relational foundation that we have already built with them in implementing the first four steps of Christ's method, helps them become receptive to Christ. They have already experienced our sympathy and love in ministering to their needs, and thereby winning their trust. Second, our altruistic motives and genuine love, something they do not find in our self-centered world, has impressed and influenced them. They desire to know why we are what we are. Third, probably they have already learned, directly or indirectly, about Christ, the Bible, the church, etc., during the course of our friendship with them. Fourth, it naturally follows that inviting them to follow Jesus is the natural outgrowth of what has already taken place.

Having been pleasantly surprised to find Christians in their world who genuinely care, they become curious as to why we operate on a different relationship than what they are accustomed to. We need to honestly tell them that whatever expression of sympathy, love, and caring they have received, it all comes from Christ, the source of all good things. By giving Him full credit, we acknowledge that without Him we are all basically self-centered.

In case we have not yet given our complete personal testimony, it is time to do just that and simultaneously invite them to join us in following Jesus, our best friend. Such testimony should not come as a surprise to them, but as something they anticipate and understand. Something that reconfirms in their minds the reason and source for our meaningful and authentic relationship with them. Of course the testimony should not be canned or rigid, but must be spontaneous and gauged to their particular needs.

But that is what following Christ produces. When we

experience Him working in and through our lives, we will have just the right and worthwhile thing to say. Ellen White writes that "as witnesses for Christ, we are to tell what we know, what we ourselves have seen and heard and felt. If we have been following Jesus step by step, we shall have something right to the point to tell concerning the way in which He has led us" (*ibid.*, p. 340). Then she underscores how urgently essential such a personal testimony is by stating that "this is the witness for which our Lord calls, and for want of which the world is perishing" (*ibid.*).

We can never overemphasize the importance and potency of a genuine and heartfelt testimony. It can transcend theoretical arguments and theological debates, and more than anything else it can move the human heart to respond to Christ. A young pastor took me along to help him with an obstinate man he was witnessing to. He explained that the wife had already accepted Christ, but the husband was holding out, raising questions about the existence of God and so forth. On the way to the man's home, I asked, "What do you really think is the problem?"

"I think I am spending too much time debating with him complicated theological arguments," he candidly responded. As he drove on, we discussed and prayed. "I really feel impressed to just go in there and give this man my simple testimony," the pastor concluded. "No big debates or arguments this time, just my testimony of what Christ has done in my life."

After greeting the man, he began, "John, you and I have been discussing various issues for quite some time now. But today I'd like to take a few minutes to share my personal testimony with you." John listened intently as the pastor opened his heart to him and explained the difference Christ's love had made in his life. It was amazing to watch the previously argumentative man raptly listening. Clearly, Christ's love manifested in the pastor's testimony was softening his heart. Finally, sobbing, John asked Christ to forgive all his sins and come into his life.

No wonder Ellen White wrote that "our confession of His faithfulness is Heaven's chosen agency for revealing Christ to the world. We are to acknowledge His grace as made known through the holy men of old; but that which will be most effectual is the testimony of our own experience." And when such personal testimonies are "supported by a Christlike life [they] have an irresistible power that works for the salvation of souls" (*ibid.*, p. 347).

We can share our personal testimony in many different ways, but we should never present it in a rushed, memorized, or mechanical way, attempting to produce instant conversion. That does not mean that we need not think through what we plan to say ahead of time. It might even be advisable for some to write out their testimonies in full, while maintaining enough flexibility to remain spontaneous and sensitive to the particular needs of each situation. What is of vital importance is that "the gospel is to be presented, not as a lifeless theory, but as a living force to change the life" (*The Ministry of Healing,* p. 99).

What do we say or include in our testimony? We find the answer in what Jesus asked the demoniac, whom He had just healed, to do. "Go home to your friends, and tell them how much the Lord has done for you, and how he has had mercy on you" (Mark 5:19). The people of his city knew all too well about his past life, so he did not need to dwell on that. Rather, Jesus wanted him to emphasize how he had met the Lord, and what the Lord had wrought in his life. It does not mean that we should remain silent about our past life, but it should not be the focus of our testimony, especially if it might contain some sensational incidents or gory details. The purpose of any personal testimony is never to glamorize sin, but to glorify Jesus.

The apostle Paul's testimony to his fellow Jews upon his return to Jerusalem may serve as a useful example in preparing our own. We can glean from the record in Acts 22 four main components. First, a sketch of his life before Christ entered it. Second, how he became a follower of Christ. Third, what Christ had been doing in his life after the Damascus road experience (in our case, our conversions). Finally, his outlook for the future as a result of following Christ.

Using the four main points, we should prepare the general outline of what we want to say. It should not be lengthy or cumbersome, but fragrant and palpating with Christ's presence in our lives.

CHRIST'S WAY OF REACHING PEOPLE

We must remember that although it is helpful to have a polished testimony, what makes it really effective is revealing Christ as a living reality in our daily lives. The power of such a Christlike life can even take an awkwardly presented testimony and cause it to change lives. "Our influence upon others depends not so much upon what we say as upon what we are. Men may combat and defy our logic, they may resist our appeals; but a life of disinterested love is an argument they cannot gainsay. A consistent life, characterized by the meekness of Christ, is a power in the world" (*The Desire of Ages,* p. 142).

When we invite persons to accept Christ, do we lead them to follow Him either as Saviour or Lord, or both as Saviour and Lord? Some witnesses will emphasize only Jesus' love and redemption, or on the other hand, only His obedience and lordship. The word *balance* has become increasingly important to me, because it is quite easy to go to extremes in everything nowadays.

It is not a matter of either/or, but both. When we choose to follow Jesus, we need to be committed to all of Him. Christ is not divided. Either we have all of Jesus or none of Him. He is not only our Saviour but also our Lord. We not only love Him, but we also obey and serve Him. And He not only justifies us but also sanctifies us. Thus we need to not only accept Him but also follow Him "wherever he goes" (Rev. 14:4).

Many years ago my sister asked me to baby-sit my 4-year-old niece while she did some shopping. Unfortunately she was gone for several hours. In the meantime the child got hungry and wanted me to feed her lunch. Not being a cook, I resorted to what I best knew how to make: sandwiches—in this case, a peanut butter and jelly sandwich. I spread some sweet jelly and creamy peanut butter on two slices of whole-wheat bread and gave it to her.

A few minutes later as I checked to see how she was getting along, I discovered that she had scraped off the jelly and peanut butter, swallowed it, and discarded the slices of bread. Whenever I recall that experience, I think of how often many of us are like my little niece. We crave the sweetness of the gospel but discard its substance.

FOLLOW ME

When we explain a balanced and complete concept of following Christ to our friends, and they heartily accept it, committing themselves to Him as the Saviour and Lord of their lives, then they are ready for Bible studies for two reasons. First, such studies are rooted in a solid relational foundation with us. We are already good friends with them. And second, they are anchored in a solid relational foundation with Christ. They have already chosen to follow Him as Saviour and Lord.

On the other hand, if we have not helped them to establish a secure relational foundation with us and Christ, then our whole structure of discipling them can crumble at any time. Why? Because none of us have invested in the relationship. Yes, they have heard some theoretical ideas and have been presented with a program, but the emphasis on the person and the process was lacking. That is why they sometimes tell us that they do not want to continue the Bible studies. They feel they do not have much to lose in a friendship or a relationship with us and the Lord, for they did not have any to begin with.

However, if we have been implementing the steps of Christ's method, they will want to grow in their knowledge of the One they love, and also please Him in all things. Paul and Jesus affirm repeatedly this important principle.

The apostle combines the ever-growing experience of knowing Christ with the ever-advancing life of obedience to Him. For instance, he writes to the Colossians, "You are living a brand new kind of life that is continually learning more and more of what is right, and trying constantly to be more and more like Christ who created this new life within you" (Col. 3:10, TLB). And "asking that the way you live will always please the Lord and honor him . . . while all the time you are learning to know God better and better" (Col. 1:10, TLB).

Christ said in John 14:15, "If you love me, you will keep my commandments."

One of the first Bible studies I gave was to a young man who had finally capitulated to my incessant appeals to study with him. He had grown up with quite negative ideas about God, so when I unleashed on him all the proof texts and the historical support for observing the seventh-day Sabbath instead of Sunday, he made a comment still indelibly imprinted in my mind. "You know, I cannot stand God for one minute, and now you would have me spend a whole day, from sunset to sunset, with Him!"

That is why it makes good sense to let every Bible teaching be Christ-motivated and Christ-centered. As disciples of Christ we are to make sure that everything we teach finds its focus in Him. He in Himself is the most attractive, compelling, and lasting reason for people to commit themselves to Him. Since we have already alluded to the Sabbath doctrine, let us use that as an example of our approach. What are the main and most effective reasons we need to give others for observing the Sabbath?

1. Christ from the very beginning involved Himself with man. He demonstrated His love not only by breathing life into him, but also in choosing to set aside a special day to commune with humanity.

2. Christ's love always searches for man, and seeks togetherness with him. In fact, the entire Bible is saturated with references to His intense desire to be with His people. For Jesus to establish one special day to spend with us is a concrete sign that He loves us, and that we are special to Him.

3. So because man is so important to Christ, He made the Sabbath for him, a particular day reserved just for us and set apart from the rest of the week. Consequently, since the Sabbath is so important to Christ, it follows that it must be the same way to us too.

4. The Sabbath is God's precious love gift of time to us. How do we receive a loving present from a special friend? By graciously accepting it as it is. We should do the same with Christ's gift of the Sabbath by not substituting something else for it.

5. Jesus Himself customarily worshiped on the seventh-day Sabbath. His prophets and disciples did too. Being committed to following Him, we want to live even as He did. How can we go wrong if we follow His example?

6. The Sabbath symbolizes Christ's creation and redemption of man. He rested on that day after He finished His act of creation in the garden, and He also rested on that same day when He finished His act of redemption at Golgotha.

People taking Bible studies make a commitment to follow Christ's example in every one of His teachings, so that when they come toward the end of the lessons, they will again decide to emulate Christ's example through baptism by immersion. They do not take this important step merely because they become fascinated by the doctrines in themselves, but because the Christ of all the doctrines has captivated them. Also their baptism must be a service of consecration for witnessing. Again they are following Christ's example in His baptism when the Holy Spirit anointed Him for His ministry (Luke 3:21-23).

Therefore, we help them to model after Christ in every respect, including His baptism and consecration for service. As new members of the body of Christ, they begin to witness in the same way as their friends previously demonstrated Christ to them. In other words, they reach out to people as Jesus did by applying His method of witnessing. We will be developing this topic more fully in the following chapter, "Fishers of Men." But it suffices here to quote a statement from *The Ministry of Healing:* "Every true disciple is born into the kingdom of God as a missionary. No sooner does he come to know the Saviour than he desires to make others acquainted with Him. The saving and sanctifying truth cannot be shut up in his heart" (p. 102).

When Jesus called the disciples to follow Him (Matt. 4:19), He intentionally bypassed the most educated and cultured persons and chose an unrefined and uneducated band of mostly fishermen. And for what purpose? To hold a position that "was the most important to which human beings had ever been called, and was second only to that of Christ Himself" (*The Desire of Ages,* p. 291).

What kind of qualifications did they possess? Not much by the world's standards. Christ knew well their defects before He selected them. But He was the kind of leader who took people from where they were and trained them for ministry to others. That was possible because the disciples were, not overlooking their imperfections and errors, "men of native ability, and they were humble and teachable—men whom He could educate for His work" (*ibid.*, p. 250).

Truly the best qualifications for spiritual training are humility and teachableness. And the disciples possessed these qualifications even though too few of the religious leaders of their day did. Such characteristics combined with having Jesus as their unequaled teacher for more than three years transformed them to be more like Him. And what a great teacher to have! He taught hour by hour, He continuously prayed for them, and He loved them and believed in them till the end. "When the disciples came forth from the Saviour's training, they were no longer ignorant and uncultured. They had become like Him in mind and character, and men took knowledge of them that they had been with Jesus" (*ibid.*).

We can have no greater qualifications to witness as Christ did than the two mentioned above. First, to become like Him in character, and second, to be recognized, by the way we relate to those around us, as having been with Jesus. Together they constitute the most attractive and drawing power that exists in the world. It is a power that is not self-generated, but proceeds from Christ-transformed characters, and exudes from His presence in our lives. Zechariah 8:23 vividly depicts the drawing power of a Christlike person. "In those days ten men from the nations of every tongue shall take hold of the robe of a Jew, saying, 'Let us go with you, for we have heard that God is with you.' "

We cannot possibly witness successfully except with Christ abiding in us and transforming our lives. Bonhoeffer, who certainly knew what it meant to be a disciple of Christ, said: "When we are called to follow Christ, we are summoned to an exclusive attachment to his person. . . . Discipleship means adherence to Christ" (Bonhoeffer, *The Cost of Discipleship,* p. 63). And that is precisely what Jesus emphasized in calling His disciples: "to be with him" (Mark 3:14). In Matthew 4:19 He said, "Follow me, and I will make you fishers of men." Notice that He wanted them to concentrate on being with Him, to follow Him, and not to be preoccupied with trying to make themselves into witnesses. That was *His* responsibility, not theirs.

It is crucial to keep in mind Christ's emphasis on following Him and letting Him make us witnesses. We are prone to become absorbed in ourselves and what we can accomplish, instead of simply focusing on being with Christ and letting Him transform us into the kind of witnesses He desires us to be. "We do not become effective at influencing men for Christ by concentrating on ourselves and our growing skills. Our effectiveness will never depend on that. The key will always be our immediate, personal relationship with our Lord as we follow him" (McDill, *Making Friends for Christ,* p. 108).

Peter finally learned the essential lesson of following. Christ lovingly and patiently taught him the need to cling constantly to Him. The disciple had been impetuous, aggressive, self-confident, and ambitious. Until then "Peter had been inclined to act independently. He had tried to plan for the work of God, instead of waiting to follow out God's plan. But he could gain nothing by rushing on before the Lord. Jesus bids him, 'Follow Me.' Do not run ahead of Me" (*The Desire of Ages,* p. 816). Happily, Peter, because of his attitude of teachableness, trust, and love of Christ, emerged from the Master's hand molded, transformed, and firmly anchored in Him.

A preacher related how he enjoyed strolling along the beach collecting the shells tossed here and there by the waves. As he wandered along, selecting the better shells, he noticed one that he wanted in his collection. It had settled on a big rock nearby. Reaching for it, he discovered it was stuck to the rock. When he tried again with both hands, it simply would not budge. Apparently it was so embedded in the rock that it was as impossible to dislodge it as to move the rock itself. Likewise with all the Peters called to follow Christ. They begin as pebbles and shells tossed back and forth by the waves and circumstances of life. However, when they tenaciously cleave to Christ the solid Rock, they become one with Him, immovable.

FISHERS OF MEN

"Now it came to pass," begins the parable composed by John Drescher, "that a group existed who called themselves fishermen. And lo, there were many fish in the waters all around. In fact the whole area was surrounded by streams and lakes filled with fish. And the fish were hungry.

"Week after week, month after month, and year after year these, who called themselves fishermen, met in meetings and talked about their call to fish, the abundance of fish, and how they might go about fishing. Year after year they carefully defined what fishing means, defended fishing as an occupation, and declared that fishing is always to be a primary task of fishermen.

"Continually they searched for new and better methods of fishing and for new and better definitions of fishing. Further, they said, 'The fishing industry exists by fishing, as fire exists by burning.' They loved slogans such as 'Fishing is the task of every fisherman,' 'Every fisherman is a fisher,' and 'A fisherman's outpost for every fisherman's club.' They sponsored special meetings called 'Fishermen's Campaigns,' and 'The Month for Fishermen to Fish.' They sponsored costly nationwide and worldwide congresses to discuss fishing and to promote fishing and hear about all the ways of fishing such as the new fishing equipment, fish calls, and whether any new bait was discovered.

FISHERS OF MEN

"These fishermen built large, beautiful buildings called 'Fishing Headquarters.' The plea was that everyone should be a fisherman and every fisherman should fish. One thing they didn't do, however; they didn't fish.

"In addition to meeting regularly, they organized a board to send out fishermen to other places where there were many fish. All the fishermen seemed to agree that what is needed is a board that could challenge fishermen to be faithful in fishing. The board was formed by those who had the great vision and courage to speak about fishing, to define fishing, and to promote the idea of fishing in faraway streams and lakes where many other fish of different colors lived.

"Also the board hired staffs and appointed committees and held many meetings to define fishing, to defend fishing, and to decide what new streams should be thought about. But the staff and committee members did not fish.

"Large, elaborate, and expensive training centers were built whose original and primary purpose was to teach fishermen how to fish. Over the years courses were offered on the needs of fish, the nature of fish, where to find fish, the psychological reactions of fish, and how to approach and feed fish. Those who taught had doctorates in fishology. But the teachers did not fish. They only taught fishing. Year after year, after tedious training, many were graduated and were given fishing licenses. They were sent to do full-time fishing, some to distant waters that were filled with fish.

"Some spent much study and travel to learn the history of fishing and to see faraway places where the founding fathers did great fishing in the centuries past. They lauded the faithful fishermen of years before who handed down the idea of fishing.

"Further, the fishermen built large printing houses to publish fishing guides. Presses were kept busy day and night to produce materials solely devoted to fishing methods, equipment, and programs to arrange and to encourage meetings to talk about fishing. A speakers' bureau was also provided to schedule special speakers on the subject of fishing.

"Many who felt the call to be fishermen responded. They were commissioned and sent to fish. But like the fishermen back home, they never fished. Like the fishermen back home, they engaged in all kinds of other occupations. They built power plants to pump water for fish and tractors to plow new waterways. They made all kinds of equipment to travel here and there to look at fish hatcheries. Some also said that they wanted to be part of the fishing party, but they felt called to furnish fishing equipment. Others felt that their job was to relate to the fish in a good way so the fish would know the difference between good and bad fishermen. Others felt that simply letting the fish know they were nice, land-loving neighbors and how loving and kind they were was enough.

"After one stirring meeting on 'The Necessity for Fishing,' one young fellow left the meeting and went fishing. The next day he reported that he had caught two outstanding fish. He was honored for his excellent catch and was scheduled to visit all the big meetings possible to tell how he did it. So he quit his fishing in order to have time to tell about the experience to the other fishermen. He was also placed on the fishermen's General Board as a person having considerable experience.

"Now it's true that many of the fishermen sacrificed and put up with all kinds of difficulties. Some lived near the water and bore the smell of dead fish every day. They received the ridicule of some who made fun of their fishermen's clubs and the fact that they claimed to be fishermen yet never fished. They wondered about those who felt it was of little use to attend the weekly meetings to talk about fishing. After all, were they not following the Master, who said, 'Follow me, and I will make you fishers of men'?

"Imagine how hurt some were when one day a person suggested that those who don't catch fish were really not fishermen, no matter how much they claimed to be. Yet it did sound correct. Is a person a fisherman if year after year he never catches a fish? Is one following if he isn't fishing?" ("A Fish Story," *Ministry* [April 1979], p. 9).

And we can answer Drescher's question with a resounding "No, one is not!" He is quite right that there can be no following without fishing. But also we need to add that there can be no fishing without following. Following Christ and fishing with Christ are inextricably bound up with each other. The two really are so intertwined that they cannot exist apart separately. What we need to be constantly aware of is how subtle and easy it is to imagine that we can have one without the other.

Some Christians think they can merely follow Christ without serving Him. Preoccupied with trying to be spiritual, studying, and attending religious meetings, they complacently receive God's blessings yet shrink from sharing them with others. "Those who endeavor to maintain Christian life by passively accepting the blessings that come through the means of grace, and doing nothing for Christ, are simply trying to live by eating without working" (*Steps to Christ,* pp. 80, 81).

They claim that their silent witness, their good example, is all that God expects. Of course a good example is vital, but that is not sufficient. Besides that, our inner experience must give concrete outer expression in speaking and doing. Just as we must sprinkle the salt on the food, likewise we are to go after the fish. Christ's great love in our hearts cannot leave us passive, but it gives us a burning and urgent desire to reach out to the lost. For example when the prophet Jeremiah thought he could silence his witness, he found it impossible. "If I say, 'I will not mention him, or speak anymore in his name,' there is in my heart as it were a burning fire shut up in my bones, and I am weary with holding it in, and I cannot" (Jer. 20:9).

Fish and Conant admit that too many Christians who believe in witnessing to others do not go about it the right way, unfortunately. The authors put it well when they comment about such silent-witness Christians: "They had done their utmost to get the sheaves to come in out of the field and be harvested; to get the fish to come to shore and be caught; to get the dead to come after life" (*Every-Member Evangelism,* p. 34). Then they challenge, "The harvest is dead ripe and ready to be harvested while the harvesters are sitting in the storehouse, wondering why it doesn't come in! The harvest can be gathered as soon as the harvesters go into the field after it!" (*ibid.,* p. 35).

But then we have the other extreme of making a god of our frantic external witnessing activities and programs while neglecting the inward witness. Such individuals are probably trying to fill the void left from not following and being filled with Christ.

109

In other words, we become so engrossed in doing the Lord's work, that we forget about the Lord.

No one is really immune from the danger. It was not only the rabbis of Christ's day who succumbed to the condition, but the disciples as well. "In the estimation of the rabbis it was the sum of religion to be always in a bustle of activity. They depended upon some outward performance to show their superior piety . . . The same dangers still exist. As activity increases and men become successful in doing any work for God, there is danger of trusting to human plans and methods. There is a tendency to pray less, and to have less faith. Like the disciples, we are in danger of losing sight of our dependence on God, and seeking to make a savior of our activity" (*The Desire of Ages,* p. 362).

Ellen White endeavors to balance and blend the two essentials of witnessing: being with Christ, and working for Christ. She counsels us to (1) "look constantly to Jesus," and (2) "take time for meditation, for prayer, and for the study of the Word of God." At the same time we recognize that (1) "it is His power which does the work," and (2) "we are to labor earnestly for the salvation of the lost" (*ibid.*). Then she concludes, "Only the work accomplished with much prayer, and sanctified by the merit of Christ, will in the end prove to have been efficient for good" (*ibid.*).

Obviously Jesus followed a balanced concept of not only *being* but also *doing* in witnessing. For to His disciples He said not only "follow me" but also "I will make you fishers of men" (Matt. 4:19). We all have encountered Christians who take either the first or the second part of the verse and run with it. But the two aspects must go hand in hand. Jesus asked them to replace their occupation of literal fishing with the vocation of fishing for people. In other words, He was not calling them to follow Him as an end in itself, but to witness to others.

But what are the stipulations for becoming fishers of men? First, we need to make ourselves available to Christ by accepting His invitation to come to Him. Are we willing to wholeheartedly present ourselves to Him? Second, we need to submit to Christ so that He may fashion us according to His will. The verb *to make* in Matthew 4:19 has a rich spiritual significance. Besides meaning to form, to fashion, or to create, it can also refer to kneading paste, dough, or clay in order to bring something into being. God used such moving imagery in Jeremiah 18:6 to describe His work on His people. "O house of Israel, can I not do with you as this potter has done? says the Lord. Behold, like the clay in the potter's hand, so are you in my hand, O house of Israel." In Genesis 1:27 and 2:7 God formed man out of clay into His image. Submission to Christ's creative work in us signifies humility and teachableness. Juan Ortiz, the spirited Argentinean preacher, stresses that submission to Christ should be the "first law of discipleship" and that "there is no formation without submission" (*Disciple,* p. 111).

The third stipulation for becoming fishers of men is that we must let Christ fashion us into the kind of witnesses we need to be. We just do not go about attempting to become witnesses in our own image—our own ideas, and methods. In our modern age, man is trying to make God into his image in every aspect of his life. To him God becomes an object to manipulate and use to his own selfish pursuits. It would be tragic should we, as the fishers of men, become so enticed by the glamorous ideas and plans of the world that we overlook Christ's method of witnessing.

Fourth, for Christ to make us into fishers of men calls for a miracle. In Luke 5:1-11, considering that the disciples had toiled hard all night without even catching a single fish, the overloaded net was something supernatural. Christ fashioning us into His kind of witnesses is equally an act of creation. It is His exclusive work because "apart from me," He says, "you can do nothing" (John 15:5). Therefore, let us allow Him to create us into His witnesses, and let us submit ourselves to be re-created.

Fifth, our formation into Christ's witnesses is not instantaneous. Fashioning something is a gradual process that takes time. We know that Christ's disciples did not become accomplished fishers of men overnight. It took more than three years with Christ, and even beyond that, to mature their witnessing. This, however, does not mean that they were idle during all those years with Christ. Not at all. They were learning and putting it to practice. The *Good News Bible* conveys this concept in Matthew

4:19 more clearly. "Come with me, and I will teach you to catch men." *The Living Bible* paraphrases it, "Come along with me and I will show you how to fish for the souls of men."

We are Christ's construction project, and He is continually working toward its completion. The apostle Paul confidently assured the Philippian Christians that He "who began a good work in you will carry it on to completion until the day of Christ Jesus" (Phil. 1:6, NIV). Moreover, Ellen White describes our gradual process of training as "apprenticeship to Christ" and as "divine instruction." She states that "He who called the fishermen of Galilee is still calling men to His service. . . . However imperfect and sinful we may be, the Lord holds out to us the offer of partnership with Himself, of apprenticeship to Christ. He invites us to come under the divine instruction, that, uniting with Christ, we may work the works of God" (*The Desire of Ages,* p. 297).

The last stipulation, but definitely not the least, is grasping the indispensable lesson of self-distrust. Yet we must never experience self-distrust apart from Christ-trust. There must always exist an essential tension between self-distrust and Christ-trust, something that we can never assimilate from any human teacher or any human theory—only the Master Teacher Himself. "The first thing to be learned by all who would become workers together with God is the lesson of self-distrust. . . . This is not to be gained through education in the most scientific schools. It is the fruit of wisdom that is obtained from the divine Teacher alone" (*ibid.,* p. 250).

Simon Peter experienced what it meant to distrust himself and to trust Jesus when, on the shores of Lake Gennesaret, the Master Fisherman told him not to be afraid, for "henceforth you will be catching men" (Luke 5:10). An expert, Peter was thoroughly acquainted with fishing in those familiar waters. He had earned his livelihood there for most of his life. And on that particular night he had chosen the ideal spot and the ideal time in the darkness of the night to work the waters of that lake. He had labored hard all night, using every trick and every bit of expertise he had ever acquired, but to no avail. Yet as the first rays of the morning crept over the hills in the east, he had absolutely nothing to show for his efforts—not even one small fish. Not only Peter, but anyone who had done his utmost best only to experience total failure, would have been greatly disappointed. But here comes Jesus and tells him to let down his nets for a catch. Most likely that was the last thing in the world that Peter had in mind to do. Yes, he would try again for sure, but not then, just in the wake of his miserable failure.

He might have thought to himself, *Jesus, with all due respect to You, would You please leave whatever involves fishing to me? I admit that there are many things I am not good at, but at least I know fishing. Fishing is my livelihood.* And if Jesus were to respond to Peter's inner thoughts, He would have probably said, "Yes, Peter, you are indeed an expert fisherman, and you know a lot about fish. But Peter, I made the fish, and I certainly know how to gather them to the nets!"

"But at your word I will let down the nets" (Luke 5:5), Peter obediently said to Him. That kind of obedience was an authentic expression of his abiding trust and love for Jesus. His faith in the Lord received an astonishing reward, with the nets breaking and the boats sinking because of the weight of the catch. Peter, overwhelmed by the Master's great power over nature, his love for Him, and a great sense of his own unworthiness in Jesus' holy presence, threw himself at his Saviour's knees, saying, "Depart from me, for I am a sinful man, O Lord" (verse 8).

The apostle did not really want Jesus to leave him, but he felt so unworthy to be with Him. As if he were confessing, "Lord, how can You stand being around some sinful and undeserving person like me! But I need to stay close to You. Leave me, but please don't leave me!" I like the paraphrase of *The Living Bible:* "Oh, sir, please leave us—I am too much of a sinner for you to have around." And Ellen White in commenting on the incident, wrote, "Peter exclaimed, 'Depart from me; for I am a sinful man;' yet he clung to the feet of Jesus, feeling that he could not be parted from Him" (*The Desire of Ages,* p. 246).

It was immediately following Peter's simultaneous experience of self-distrust and Christ-trust that he received the call to be a fisher of men. We may organize Peter's experience, which prepared him to witness, into three parts. One, he recognized who Christ really was with all His great love, acceptance, and power. Two, in light of that, he saw a clear picture of who he really was with all his unworthiness. And three, as a result of his moving encounter with Jesus and with his true self, he experienced the essential tension between his utter trust in His Lord and his total distrust of self. He was inadequate, while Christ was totally sufficient; unworthy, while Christ was all worthy. Now, however, in Christ he became adequate and worthy to witness to others.

Consequently, we become liberated from the bondage to self and can now freely live and witness for Christ. For in Christ we do not worry about what others may think of us, but rather how He views us. Too often we expend great energy and exhaust ourselves focusing on how others regard us and our ministry. Would it not be much more profitable to redirect our precious time and energy to Christ? It would become our highest joy to work with Him and to please Him in all things. Ellen White admonishes us to "know what it is to be *free* in Christ" by explaining that we need to trust in Him, submitting our lives to Him because we are not engaged in our own work, but His (*The Ministry of Healing,* pp. 513, 514).

It also follows that "as we become interested in the salvation of souls we cease to mind the little differences that so often arise. . . . Whatever others may think of us or do to us, it need not disturb our oneness with Christ, the fellowship of the Spirit" (*ibid.*, p. 485). Then, like Christ, we will not become "elated by applause, nor dejected by censure or disappointment." And we do not strive for a high position, but we feel that the highest role that we can occupy is found in following and learning from Jesus. The true value of our witness "does not consist in making a show and noise in the world, and in being active and zealous in our own strength" (*The Desire of Ages,* pp. 330, 331).

What compels us to witness as Christ did? What factors influence and shape a Christlike approach to others? We will examine three. They pertain to Christ, others, and self.

First, let us look at what motivates us for Christ's sake. His matchless love awakens love in our hearts, and stirs us to action not because of guilt, fear, or reward, but simply because we love

Him. It is like having a good and trusted friend who has been unbelievably accepting, dependable, and helpful. Because of who he is, we find ourselves moved to do something nice for him to express our gratitude. The desire drives us not because we feel we have to, but because we really want to.

It might startle us to hear that the all-sufficient Christ needs us. Yet He has deliberately chosen to touch people's lives through our own. He could have used angels to reveal Himself before humanity, but He made Himself dependent on us human beings. Not only because He wanted to build our characters, but also because we share mutual human experiences and struggles with others. "Christ took upon Himself humanity, that He might reach humanity. Divinity needed humanity; for it required both the divine and the human to bring salvation to the world. Divinity needed humanity, that humanity might afford a channel of communication between God and man" (*ibid.*). V. W. Schoen, who was quite involved throughout his life in training church members to share their faith, wrote a book under the intriguing title *God's Need*. In it he shows how greatly God needs people to convey His love and truth to others around them (pp. 7-12).

Second, for others' sake. As we mentioned earlier, when overwhelmed with Christ's love and goodness toward us, we find ourselves overpowered with the heartfelt desire to reciprocate. We ask Him if there is something we can do for Him, and He answers, Yes, there is. But what is it? we inquire. "Assuredly, I say to you, inasmuch as you did it to one of the least of these My brethren, you did it to Me" (Matt. 25:40, NKJV). Note that this is the only criterion that Christ states He will employ in determining who will be saved or lost at His second coming. In Matthew 25:35, 36, He does not use any theological arguments, or anything else for that matter, except how we treat people.

Christ cites six specific examples of how we conduct ourselves toward people who are hungry, thirsty, strangers, naked, sick, and in prison. In being kind, loving, and helpful to others, we are in reality doing it to Christ *Himself!* Mother Teresa of Calcutta has declared that in caring for the poorest of the poor, and in loving the least of the least, she is in fact caring for and loving Jesus Himself.

CHRIST'S WAY OF REACHING PEOPLE

And whenever I hear Mother Teresa speak of "the poorest of the poor," I become painfully aware of the shallow and even empty claims that we make about truly loving Jesus. Her words, and Jesus' comment about "the least of these," convict us that we do not love Jesus as much as we do the lovable and lovely, but rather at the level of those whom we consider the lowest. Let us think for a moment of a person we have little or no feeling for. Now as we have that particular person in mind, let the thought sink in that we have the same love for Jesus as we have for that individual.

It is quite revealing that the righteous, in reaching out in love to the people around them, were totally unaware that they were doing it to Jesus, or that their caring acts had any bearing on their eternal salvation (Matt. 25:37-39). The fact that Jesus' commendations startled them clearly tells us about their true nature. They did not let the prospect of reward or punishment or any other self-serving incentive motivate them, but were simply and genuinely compelled by their love of their neighbors. They were mingling with others—like Jesus—as ones desiring their good, for their own sake.

One Bible commentary explains that Jesus' reference to His brethren refers to "any human beings who are in need. To receive such a one is to receive Christ; to refuse to aid such a one is to refuse Christ." Then it points out the only motive the righteous really have for helping the needy around them. "The surprising element in this parable-like description of the judgment is that those who are welcomed into the kingdom have had no consciousness that the acts of mercy they performed had any relationship to Christ, much less to their eternal destiny. They acted because their fellow man was in need, not in order to earn a reward or to merit admission to the kingdom" (Charles M. Laymon, ed., *The Interpreter's One-Volume Commentary on the Bible,* p. 640).

The last time Jesus talked with Peter, He met him by the Sea of Tiberias, where he and the other disciples were at it again —fishing. After he finished the breakfast Jesus had prepared them, Peter pondered the most important question ever addressed to him. It was so vital that Christ asked it three times: "Simon, son of John, do you love me more than these?'' (John 21:15-17).

And when Peter responded in the affirmative, Jesus immediately said to him, ''Feed my sheep.'' We observe a definite link between Peter's love for Christ and his love for His sheep. Christ wanted the disciple to know that his service to others must be motivated by His love. In other words, our motivation of love in witnessing—in feeding and tending the sheep—is a tangible expression of His love to us. Our horizontal level of reaching out in love to others springs forth from the vertical level of His love to us.

If we honestly examined the intents of our hearts, what motives and drives would we find there? Are our expressions of love conditional? Do we find ourselves parceling out our love to some but not to others? Ellen White refers to our unconditional love, which enfolds all human beings, as ''the insignia of the royalty of heaven.'' Says she, ''It is not earthly rank, nor birth, nor nationality, nor religious privilege, which proves that we are members of the family of God; it is love, a love that embraces all humanity. . . . To be kind to the unthankful and to the evil, to do good hoping for nothing again, is the insignia of the royalty of heaven, the sure token by which the children of the Highest reveal their high estate'' (*Thoughts From the Mount of Blessing,* p. 75). Moreover, ''When love fills the heart, it will flow out to others, not because of favors received from them, but because love is the principle of action'' (*ibid.,* p. 38). The sheep, whom Jesus wants us to draw to Him and to love unconditionally, are not just the ones already in the fold, but also those outside it (John 10:16). Therefore, it involves our inreach as well as our outreach activities. Both activities must always be united, and are fruitless if they are not. Lenard Jaecks compares it to breathing. He asks, ''How can you separate inhaling (inreach) from exhaling (outreach)? They are both ingredients of one activity'' (Lenard D. Jaecks, ''Adventists Involved in the 'Shut Door' Again,'' *Gleaner,* Dec. 18, 1989, p. 6).

Third, for our sake. I am sure that you will agree that our Christian experience becomes alive and vibrant when we reach out to others around us. I will never forget the change that would take place when I would involve young people in witnessing for

Christ. Often their critical and self-centered attitudes would change as a result of seeing what problems other people had, and by helping and praying for them. Point to me a person or a church that is spiritually alive, and I will show you a person or a church active in witnessing. Christ could have given this responsibility to angels, but in His love He knew that participating in saving others would bring us closest to Him. "Those who thus become participants in labors of love are brought nearest to their Creator" (*Steps to Christ,* p. 79).

Let us summarize the personal, spiritual benefits of following Christ's example in witnessing:

1. We witness for our very spiritual survival. If we do not share what we have, we lose it. We become spiritually stagnant, weak, and eventually die. Personal witnessing is like physical activity. What would happen if we ate and slept but did not exercise our bodies? Gradually we would become obese, weak, and sickly. "A man who would refuse to exercise his limbs would soon lose all power to use them. Thus the Christian who will not exercise his God-given powers not only fails to grow up into Christ, but he loses the strength that he already had" (*Steps to Christ,* p. 81).

2. As we witness we grow in Christ's love. It is true that when we do not get involved with people, sympathize with them, help them, and pray for them, our love for Christ and for them grows cold. As the saying goes, "Out of sight, out of mind." "Visit your neighbors in a friendly way, and become acquainted with them. . . . Those who do not take up this work, those who act with the indifference that some have manifested, will soon lose their first love, and will begin to censure, criticize, and condemn their own brethren" (*Christian Service,* p. 115).

3. Witnessing will overcome our self-centeredness. Nobody can touch the lives of other people, feel their pain, think of them, and pray for them while remaining self-centered. In fact some might purposely not want to get involved in witnessing because they realize it would compel them to abandon their cozy selfishness.

4. Our knowledge of the Bible and spiritual things will increase. The persons we witness to will ask questions, and seek

our suggestions in dealing with their problems. That in itself will drive us to the Bible and to prayer seeking God's wisdom. "If you go to work as Christ designs that His disciples shall, and win souls for Him, you will feel the need of a deeper experience and a greater knowledge in divine things. . . . Encountering opposition and trials will drive you to the Bible and prayer" (*Steps to Christ*, p. 80).

5. Personal witnessing brings about spiritual maturity. "The spirit of unselfish labor for others gives depth, stability, and Christlike loveliness to the character. . . ." Those who seek the salvation of others will become strong in the Lord, and "they will have clear spiritual perceptions, a steady, growing faith, and an increased power in prayer" (*ibid.*).

6. Christ uses witnessing to bring us closest to Him (*ibid.*, p. 79). Why? Because we are involved in our Saviour's most important and cherished work—that of saving others. In His love for lost humanity, He went to the extreme of dying on the cross to bring salvation.

7. Finally, becoming mature witnesses for Christ will lead us to demonstrate to others how to witness. That will in turn help them to stay alive spiritually. Once I heard it said, "Give someone a fish and he will live for a day, but teach someone how to fish and he will live for a lifetime." And in a spiritual sense, live eternally. Robert Coleman asked, "How else will His way ever be learned? It is well enough to tell people what we mean, but it is infinitely better to show them how to do it. People are looking for a demonstration, not an explanation" (*The Master Plan of Evangelism*, p. 80).

Someone once asked me why Jesus had used the expression "fishers of men" in describing His witnesses. "Does not that imply trickery, deception, and entrapment?" he wondered. "You see, fishing involves nets, hooks, baits, and coercion. Could not Jesus have used a better expression for conveying what true personal witnessing is all about?" They are good questions that many sincere people raise. Let us try to answer them by presenting the following suggestions:

First of all, I do not believe that Jesus had any inclination or bias toward the fishing profession. He simply met people on their level and tried to channel their temporal interests into eternal ones. Furthermore, we need to remember that Jesus' reference to being "fishers of men" was primarily an illustration, an analogy to point to greater spiritual realities. Therefore, we need to take it as such, and not analyze each point of the comparison literally.

The disciples happened to be fishermen by profession, so Jesus called them to go beyond catching fish for themselves to attracting people to Himself. It is certainly not unreasonable to conclude that if the disciples had happened to be shepherds, Jesus would have called them to be shepherds of men, or to feed His sheep as He commissioned Peter to do (John 21:15-17). Or if the disciples had worked on farms, He would have called them to be harvesters of souls, and so on.

Second, many automatically think of bait and hook when they consider the topic of fishing, thereby conjuring up the negative connotations of deceit and ensnarement. However, the disciples did not fish with bait or hook for sport as many do today, but used a net. When Jesus performed the miracle of filling their nets with fish, He demonstrated His ability not merely to gather the fish of the sea, but more significantly to draw and gather human beings to Himself. Therefore, the lesson that Jesus intended for us to learn from His illustration of fishing is His ability, manifested through our availability, to attract many people to Him.

But still there are some who, because they vehemently oppose fishing (witnessing) by hook, insist that we should never have any ulterior motives—or any motives whatsoever—in witnessing to others. We can certainly understand such a point of view because so many do try to manipulate and coerce others in the name of religion. But, in our zeal, we must be careful not to throw the baby out with the bathwater. We must always be motivated by love, yet equally concerned to see those whom Jesus died for be eternally saved rather than eternally lost.

There is absolutely nothing wrong with such motives. In fact, something terrible would be wrong in our Christian experience if we did not have such compelling reasons for our witnessing. Christ journeyed to our hopeless world because of His love and concern for our salvation. In His great love He "came to seek and to save the lost" (Luke 19:10). His motivation must be ours too. If we reach out to others without Christ's loving desire to save them from destruction, we would prove that our own love for them is deficient, and at best shortsighted.

Third, in studying the meaning of the Greek verb *zogreo* used by Christ in Luke 5:10 and rendered "to catch men" in English, we learn that it comes from combining two Greek words: *zoos,* which means "alive," and *agreuo,* "to catch." Therefore, we could best translate *zogreo* as "to catch alive," or "to take alive." Christ, in calling Peter and the disciples to catch men, and to capture them alive, intended to show the contrast between catching fish and catching people.

Obviously, fish, forcibly dragged to shore, eventually die there. However, when we draw people out from the turbulent waters of the world to Christ, they will not perish like fish out of water, but will live and thrive. He will not just merely allow them to exist, but He will give them abundant life. They will not suffocate for lack of oxygen, but will breathe the air of Jesus' love and fellowship demonstrated in our lives and in our churches. Notice the contrast again in John 10:10. Jesus said, "The thief does not come except to steal, and to kill, and to destroy. I have come that they may have life, and that they may have it more abundantly" (NKJV).

Finally, Christ's method of witnessing results in enhanced life here and eternal life at His coming. On the other hand, baits deceive, and hooks coerce, hurt, and kill. People are to be drawn by the genuine love of Christ revealed in our lives, not roped in by our pretense and craftiness. Dr. Paul Tournier, as he clarified some Christians' misconception about being fishers of men and commented on the key to his success in drawing others to Christ, wrote, "After all, no one wants to be caught by somebody else. So I sit by the bank without a fishing pole in my hand and enjoy the scenery. Fish seem to sense that I'm not trying to catch them. They come to me just to talk about themselves and about life. Then from time to time, some do get caught by Jesus Christ and I am more surprised than they are" (in Larson, *Ask Me to Dance,* p. 32).

While we do not have to hold fishing poles in our hands, we

do not need to remain empty-handed, however. We should use a lifeline instead of a fishing line. Or we need to throw them a lifesaver while praying for them, appealing to them, and persuading them in the most attractive terms to choose to grab it, to choose life. The lifesaver does not mislead or force anyone. It is there to be chosen or rejected. But we must not make it difficult for drowning individuals to grasp it. And even more important, we need to jump into their troubled waters and help their weak hands get a hold of that lifesaver.

Matthew and Linda were a young married couple with whom I had the privilege of studying the Bible for several months. In the process of our fellowship and study we became good friends, thanks to Christ's method. But for some unknown reason, they did not seem to be interested in attending church even once, not to mention getting baptized. Finally they confided that they could not make themselves come because they did not want to get hooked.

They actually thought that if they showed up once, everybody would expect them to continue attending. And if they stopped, we would have been disappointed in them and would have terminated the friendship. They appreciated our Christian love and friendship so much that they did not want in any way to undermine that relationship. I assured them that we would never react in the way that they feared we would. "Do you mean to say that we can try it once," Matthew asked in surprise, "and if for some reason it doesn't work out, then we could stop attending?"

"Of course," I responded.

"And that would in no way affect our friendship?"

"No, not at all."

They both started going to church and soon enjoyed the services and the fellowship. But only God knew why they did not decide to be baptized at that time. We simply believed that we should place the matter in His hands and trust Him to accomplish His will in our friends' lives.

We moved away later that year, and several years passed before we heard anything from them. But a few months ago, to our pleasant surprise, we learned that they had been recently baptized, and were active in sharing their faith. The crucial factor in their decision, they emphasized, was the fact that we accepted and loved them regardless. It is true, isn't it, that the people with whom we come in touch ultimately respond more to how we relate to them than by what we may claim?

CHAPTER

TEN

—

A STRATEGY
OF REPRODUCTION

Juan Ortiz compares the multiplication of disciples to the rapid growth in population with each succeeding generation. He relates a conversation he had with an old grandmother. "This is my granddaughter," the woman said.

"Is that so?" Ortiz replied.

"Yes, I have great-grandchildren. One of them is 15 already, so if she marries soon, I may have great-great-grandchildren."

"How many children did you have?"

"Six."

"And now you have how many grandchildren?"

"Thirty-six."

"And how many great-grandchildren?"

"Who knows? I've never counted them" (*Disciple,* pp. 102, 103).

Ortiz calculates that "according to that proportion, she could have 216 great-grandchildren and 1,296 great-great-grandchildren!" Then he concludes that if he had asked her, "How did you manage such a large family—all these well-fed, well-dressed, well-educated people?" she would have replied, "I didn't. I just took care of the six." And each of them took care of their own six (*ibid.,* p. 103).

124

A STRATEGY OF REPRODUCTION

Jesus was a great believer in this principle of spiritual reproduction and growth. That is why, for more than three years, He concentrated on training His disciples in order to reproduce His life and ministry in theirs. They in turn would foster that likeness in an ever enlarging multitude of witnesses that would encircle the then known world. The term *Christian* refers to being a disciple of Christ, one who is like Christ. As Martin Luther said, Christians are to be "little Christs."

So what is a disciple of Christ who has learned to be a fisher of men? "A disciple is a person who learns to live the life his teacher lives. And gradually he teaches others to live the life he lives. . . . Discipleship is more than getting to know what the teacher knows. It is getting to be what he is" (*ibid.*). Then Ortiz explains why and how Christ commissioned His disciples to make other disciples. He did not merely want to make them witnesses; He was interested in duplicating Himself in them (*ibid.*, p. 106).

So, in a sense, we are to become duplicates of Christ the Model, and consequently, others will become models of Christ in the same manner in an ever-widening circle. "Jesus was not satisfied in having a succession of audiences to which He might proclaim His Gospel; He was interested primarily in having disciples in whom and through whom His ministry would be multiplied many times over" (James D. Smart, in Oscar Feucht, *Everyone a Minister,* p. 25). That is the reason why Christ's small handful of disciples saturated the Roman Empire with the gospel, and shook it to its very foundation. Even their enemies had to admit that they turned the whole world upside down for Christ.

The apostle Paul gives us an excellent example of this concept in 1 Corinthians 11:1. There he links his modeling after Christ to others patterning themselves after him. He writes, "Be imitators of me, as I am of Christ." Moreover, in Galatians 2:20 he fittingly describes how Christ lives out His life through him. "I have been crucified with Christ; it is no longer I who live, but Christ who lives in me." And as a result of his profound experience with Christ he invites others, in confidence and humility, to imitate him. "Brethren," he writes to the Philippians, "join in imitating me, and mark those who so live as you have an example in us" (Phil. 3:17).

Then Paul's idea of spiritual reproduction comes clearly through his admonition to the Corinthians. It corresponds to Ortiz's illustration of generational increase. Paul addresses them as his beloved children whom he had not merely shepherded, but much more significantly, he had fathered in Christ. "For though you have countless guides in Christ, you do not have many fathers. For I became your father in Christ Jesus through the gospel. I urge you, then, be imitators of me" (1 Cor. 4:14-16).

Furthermore, Christ affirms that there can be no growth in the size of the family of God unless we die to self and live for Him. "Truly, truly, I say to you, unless a grain of wheat falls into the earth and dies, it remains alone; but if it dies, it bears much fruit" (John 12:24). Hence, it is at the point of our death to self that Christ lives His life unimpeded in and through us. Death, resurrection, fruitage. In other words, our crucified life in Him becomes empowered by His resurrected life in us, resulting in great growth and fruitage.

But some may wonder how it is possible to duplicate ourselves into an ever expanding number of disciples who live out Christ's life and method of witnessing to others. Looking around us, we find ourselves puzzled as to where such potential disciples will come from. Actually they are everywhere. But the crucial issue is whether we discern the possibilities in each person. I believe that many would get involved if they had someone who would take them by the hand and show them how to do it. Ellen White tells us that "many would be willing to work if they were taught how to begin" (*Christian Service,* p. 59).

There is such a great need to show by example how to witness as Jesus did. We should not just teach others about witnessing, but we should demonstrate in practical ways how it actually occurs. Potential witnesses need to have a feel for what it is like to minister to others. Many may be somewhat hesitant or apprehensive at the beginning, but that is to be expected—they are simply worried about the unknown. However, when they come along with us and experience what it is like to help others, their fear not only evaporates, but their interest awakens as they experience for themselves how rewarding it is.

Often I encourage others to come along with me to visit or give Bible studies in homes. I remember the time when I invited a high school student to accompany me. "Tom, I am visiting and studying with a nice family, and I am looking for someone to come along for moral support," I began, "and I thought of you. I'd be very pleased to have you join me."

"No, not me!" he protested.

"And why not?"

"Well, you see, I just don't know how to witness. I don't think I ever witnessed to anyone before in my life."

"But Tom, you won't have to do a thing, because I'll do everything. You just come along and observe—that is all," I reassured him.

"You mean I'll not have to say anything!"

"That's exactly right. Just come along to pray for me and to give me some moral support."

"OK, then," he agreed. "If that's the case, let's do it." Tom not only enjoyed his first visit as he became acquainted with the spiritual needs of this family, but he kept talking about the experience all the way back to school. He was thinking of ways to help them, and he definitely wanted to go back with me the following week.

I am firmly convinced that there are many Christians like Tom—many more than we think—who would enjoy witnessing and would be spiritually revitalized if someone would only show them how. Not only are we quite lax in demonstrating how to reach others, but even worse, we sometimes dampen their enthusiasm to witness. Perhaps we are afraid they might make some mistakes. But that's how we all learn. Making mistakes can be our greatest teacher. How else can someone learn how to swim other than by getting wet, swallowing some water, and struggling to stay afloat? There is just no other way.

"If men in humble life were encouraged to do all the good they could do, if restraining hands were not laid upon them to repress their zeal there would be a hundred workers for Christ where now there is one" (*The Desire of Ages*, p. 251). She mentions an even higher ratio in *Steps to Christ,* where she writes that "if the followers of Christ were awake to duty, there would be thousands where there is one today proclaiming the gospel in heathen lands" (p. 81).

Such ratios—a hundred to one and thousands to one—not only give us great hope and confidence in how much we can accomplish, but also fill us with regret for the untold number of missed opportunities in disciple multiplication. Potential disciples are all around us, and we can have an increase of a hundred disciples witnessing for Christ instead of one if we allow Him to help us reverse this unfortunate trend.

However, the multiplication of disciples does not happen overnight. It begins small and it takes time. A hundred witnesses start with one. One faithful disciple offers himself to Christ, and the Lord takes it from there. But if we are accustomed to something big and instant, we will be disappointed. "One soul won to Christ will be instrumental in winning others, and there will be an ever-increasing result of blessing and salvation" (*Gospel Workers,* p. 184).

Moreover, it was precisely Christ's example in witnessing to the Samaritan woman. "The one soul whom He sought to help became a means of reaching others and bringing them to the Saviour. This is ever the way that the work of God has made progress on the earth. Let your light shine, and other lights will be kindled" (*ibid.*, p. 195).

Once I remember preaching a sermon on the need to witness, concluding with a rousing appeal for commitment to work for Christ. The vast majority of the church members sincerely and enthusiastically stood up with a renewed determination to witness. But predictably, and in a relatively short time, their zeal waned and the program petered out. What had gone wrong? Reflecting on that experience, I became impressed with the example of Jesus. How He emphasized the principle and potential of small, yet solid beginnings. Therefore, I prayed that He would guide me to find just one member who would be willing to come along with me, so that I might duplicate Christ's witness in his own life. That one committed individual was the beginning of a powerful nucleus of witnesses that revitalized the entire church in active service for others.

A STRATEGY OF REPRODUCTION

It would surprise us to discover how many longtime Christians would respond positively if we invited them to accompany us on our witnessing activities. Of course, on the other hand, they might turn us down, or not follow up a witnessing contact, if we were to simply give them the address and ask them to do it alone. "There are those who for a lifetime have professed to be acquainted with Christ, yet who have never made a personal effort to bring even one soul to the Saviour. They leave all the work for the minister. He may be well qualified for his calling, but he cannot do that which God has left for the members of the church" (*The Desire of Ages,* p. 141).

Using the analogy that Christ employed in John 21:15-17 when calling Peter to feed His sheep, we can say that the spiritual shepherd or overseer (see Acts 20:28) is well qualified to reproduce new sheep. However, that is not to be his primary responsibility. Rather, he is to nurture and guide the sheep, oversee their activities, equip them, and make it conducive for them to give birth to new sheep. That is the very work Christ has appointed for the sheep, and that is how the flock thrives and increases. Obviously sheep produce sheep.

John Raleigh Mott was considered a giant in the Christian world of witnessing and missions throughout his long and productive life (1865-1955). Oscar Feucht states that "it was he who gave Christendom a new vision in a single sentence: 'Greater is he that multiplies the workers than he who does the work.' " Then Feucht quotes one of the most powerful soul winners in our century, Dwight L. Moody, who said, "It's better to put 10 men to work than to do the work of 10 men" (Feucht, p. 146).

It is exciting to think of the limitless possibilities of following Christ's example. Imagine just what would happen if in each church one genuine disciple of Christ reached out to one more person and showed him how to witness. That would double his witness. And if this small nucleus of two reached out to two more, the witness would quadruple, and so on. For you see, "There is no limit to the usefulness of one who, putting self aside, makes room for the working of the Holy Spirit upon his heart and lives a life wholly consecrated to God" (*The Ministry of Healing,* p. 159).

Jesus compared the kingdom of heaven to a tiny mustard seed. It has life, and it has great potential when sown in the field. He described the mustard seed as "the smallest of all seeds, but when it has grown it is the greatest of shrubs and becomes a tree, so that the birds of the air come and make nests in its branches" (Matt. 13:32). So when Jesus established His kingdom of grace on earth, He did not begin by calling the gigantic masses to assist Him in His work, but rather was content to start with just two individuals, namely Andrew and John (see John 1:36-39).

Robert Coleman underlines Christ's example. He writes, "It did not matter how small the group was to start with so long as they reproduced, and taught their disciples to reproduce. This was the way His church was to win—through the dedicated lives of those who knew the Saviour so well that His Spirit and method constrained them to tell others. As simple as it may seem, this was the way the gospel would conquer. He had no other plan" (*The Master Plan of Evangelism,* p. 106).

Then Coleman explains that "the test of any work of evangelism thus is not what is seen at the moment, or in the conference report, but in the effectiveness with which the work continues in the next generation." Finally, he discusses the real criteria that we must use to evaluate the success of any church. Success does not depend on "how many new names are added to the roll nor how much the budget is increased, but rather how many Christians are actively winning souls and training them to win the multitudes" (*ibid.,* p. 110).

A STRATEGY OF INFILTRATION

Just as the salt pervades the food and the light penetrates the darkness, so we, as fishers of men and "duplicates" of Christ, infiltrate the world around us for Him. We become His powerful agents wherever we are, because He lives out His method of witnessing through our lives. The new persons we disciple repeat and multiply the pattern, and they in turn follow Christ and reach out to others as He did. Consequently, through us all, Christ's method will have a ripple effect in ever-expanding and increasingly powerful waves that have the potential of engulfing our homes, churches, communities, and the entire world with the gospel.

Besides the symbols of salt and light that Christ used to depict how we influence the world around us, the apostle Paul utilizes another powerful symbol. In 2 Corinthians 2:14, 15, he describes Christians as the "aroma of Christ" who spread the "fragrance of the knowledge of him everywhere." In the ancient world with its lack of sanitation, a pleasant smell was a desirable thing, and people spent fortunes on incense and perfume. The aroma of Christ was a powerful and positive symbol. Paul writes, "But thanks be to God, who in Christ always leads us in triumph, and through us spreads the fragrance of the knowledge of him everywhere. For we are the aroma of Christ to God among those who are being saved and among those who are perishing'' (2 Cor. 2:14, 15).

In studying the historical background of the preceding passage, we realize that Paul most likely had in mind a Roman triumphal procession. When a Roman general won a military victory, he would enter the gate of Rome riding in his chariot. On his head he would wear a wreath of victory, and in his hand he would hold a staff of authority. Senators, Roman officials, and citizens would meet his entourage along the way. The welcoming multitude would include incense bearers waving their censers to waft clouds of sweet fragrance. The aroma would rise and permeate the surroundings. Consequently, people would literally smell victory in the air.

Jesus is our victorious general over Satan's evil forces, and we are marching with Him in His triumphal procession, diffusing the fragrance of the gospel. The answer to all the basic questions about spreading the knowledge of Christ appears in 2 Corinthians 2:14, 15.

1. Who is the Witness par excellence? It is Jesus, who leads us as we follow.

2. What is the substance of our witness? It is Christ and the good news of His knowledge.

3. Through whom is Christ revealed? As He lives in us He spreads His knowledge through us.

4. When do we spread His good news? Always, as a way of life.

5. Where? Everywhere. Our Rome is our home, our church, our place of work, wherever we find ourselves.

What are some of the characteristics of Christ's pleasant fragrance? Spontaneous and natural, it draws and does not repulse. It is subtle, yet pervasive and powerful. As a powerful scent cannot be released or withheld at will, so ''when the love of Christ is enshrined in the heart, like sweet fragrance it cannot be hidden. Its holy influence will be felt by all with whom we come in contact'' (*Steps to Christ,* p. 77). Are we truly the aroma of Christ? Do we manifest in our lives the characteristics of His pleasant fragrance?

The fact of the matter is that we all, figuratively speaking, smell bad without the sweet fragrance of Christ pervading our lives. And His fragrance is His love enshrined in our hearts. The victorious Roman general brought along some prisoners chained to his chariot to show off as trophies of his victory. And we are Christ's trophies of His victory over Satan—not bound in fetters, but captivated by His great love that would not let go. Christ's powerful love permeates His method of witnessing, and gives our service a decisive impact on the world.

Our world starves for such genuine love, and it desperately needs Christians to diffuse it. It is the only force that can infiltrate Satan's lines and rescue lost individuals from his captivity. Even the late British philosopher Bertrand Russell, a vocal opponent of Christianity, found himself compelled to admit shortly prior to his death in 1970 what Christian love could do for the world.

He reluctantly and apologetically acknowledged that "there are certain things that our age needs. . . . The root of the matter is a thing so simple that I'm almost ashamed to mention it for fear of the derisive smile with which wise cynics will eat my words. The thing I mean—please forgive me for mentioning it—is love, Christian love, or compassion. If you feel this, you have a motive for existence, a guide in action, a reason for courage, an imperative necessity for intellectual honesty" (in Kenneth J. Holland, "Truth Must Also Move Hearts," *These Times,* Sept. 1980, p. 26).

Wayne McDill, in his work as a church growth consultant, observed four levels of approach to witnessing. First, the "verbal level," which is no more than giving lip service to outreach. Second, the "promotional level." Third, the "commitment level," where church leaders genuinely relate to outreach as a priority, planning different programs to involve the church members. And finally McDill states that he prefers the fourth level, the "overflow level" (*Making Friends for Christ,* p. 119).

"The churches expressing an overflow level of outreach thinking seem to transcend normal planning and programming and move into a different level of effectiveness. Evangelism just seems to happen. It seems as normal as breathing to the body. . . . In every church I have seen experience this overflow, the relational approach to evangelism was stressed. But beneath the apparent spontaneity was careful planning, praying, and action by church leaders'' (*ibid.*). Then he further explains the nature of the overflow level when he stresses that the ''significant penetration of the unbelieving community comes best through relational evangelism which follows normal webs of influence. Not only should lay members seek to reach present acquaintances, they should be urged to deliberately widen their circle of contacts'' (*ibid.*, p. 118).

Again using fragrance as a symbol of witnessing, we think of Mary's experience of anointing Christ's head. Her great love for Christ, borne out of her gratefulness to Him, could not be bottled up inside of her. It was like the expensive nard that she poured out over Jesus' head, thereby perfuming the whole house (see Mark 14:3-9). Naturally her response displeased Simon because he had screened his guests well, and here walked in a woman of questionable reputation. Not sure what to do exactly, he hesitated to make a scene by sending her away and thus attracting attention to her. So he simply ignored her, thinking that she would do her thing quietly, leave, and everything would go back to normal.

Of course, we know that was not what happened. Mary was absorbed with one thing: to show her great love and appreciation for Jesus. It had to be expressed. She had brought along with her a bottle of expensive nard, imported from the region of the Himalayan Mountains and worth a year's wages, and poured it on His head. The fragrance of the nard symbolized Christ's love. Quickly—to Simon's consternation—the powerful scent spread to every corner of the house. It is so true that when Christ's love fills our hearts, it—like sweet nard—just has to saturate all our surroundings.

Mary was so caught up in her ministry of love to Christ that she was oblivious to the criticism of those around her. Christ defended her. ''Let her alone,'' He said, ''why do you trouble her? She has done a beautiful thing to Me'' (Mark 14:6). It is quite significant in this connection that Jesus drew some spiritual parallels between the spreading of the nard's fragrance throughout the entire house, and the diffusion of the gospel infiltrating the entire world. Said He, ''And truly, I say to you, wherever the gospel is preached in the whole world, what she has done will be told in memory of her'' (verse 9).

As we waft the fragrance of His love and salvation every-where, we are doing ''a beautiful thing'' to Jesus Himself. And to what extent do we permeate the world with the good news? Jesus said of Mary, ''She has done what she could'' (verse 8). All He expects from us is that we do our part, no matter how small or big that might be. He just wants us to do what we can, and we can all do something for Him.

We are to be an open letter from Christ that He has inscribed in our hearts by His Spirit, and dispatched into our world ''to be known and read by all men'' (2 Cor. 3:2, 3). The crucial question for us is, What is written there in our hearts? We may tell others what the gospel is all about, but what is it according to our lives and witness? Arthur McPhee asks this pointed question: ''If you say you are a rose, and I smell a skunk, then can you blame me if I allow your words to flow in one ear and immediately out the other?'' (*Friendship Evangelism,* p. 76).

Of course, the way to smell like a rose is to bury ourselves among roses, let their scent saturate our pores. And likewise, if we want to spread the fragrance of Christ, we must immerse ourselves in Him—commune and work with Him. There is just no other way.

McPhee cites an anonymous author that captures the essence of true witnessing:

''The Gospels of Matthew, Mark, Luke and John
Are read by more than a few,
But the one that is most read and commented on
Is the gospel according to *you.*
You are writing a gospel, a chapter each day
By the things that you do and the words that you say,
Men read what you write, whether faithless or true,
Say, what is the gospel according to *you?*
Do men read His truth and His love in your life?
Or has yours been full of malice and strife?
Does your life speak of evil, or does it ring true?
Say, what is the gospel according to *you?''* (*ibid.,* pp. 76, 77).

And this is what Christ's method is all about. It is practical, transparent, uncomplicated, universal, and transcends time and place. In other words, it finds a path into the human heart regardless of background, nationality, race, education, and culture. And it does not cost much, except the giving of ourselves. With Christ's method in our hearts, heads, and hands, we can successfully infiltrate our homes, our churches, our neighborhoods, the places where we work, and make our presence felt for Him.

And we can start right now. No better or greater opportunity to reach out to others will ever come along. We often think that Christ's important ministry in behalf of others began after His baptism about the age of 30. But what about His personal witnessing while He labored as a carpenter? How are we to compare it with His later and relatively much shorter ministry of healing, teaching, and preaching? Notice what Ellen White has to say:

"The greater part of our Saviour's life on earth was spent in patient toil in the carpenter's shop at Nazareth. Ministering angels attended the Lord of life as He walked side by side with peasants and laborers, unrecognized and unhonored. He was as faithfully fulfilling His mission while working at His humble trade as when He healed the sick or walked upon the storm-tossed waves of Galilee. So in the humblest duties and lowliest positions of life, we may walk and work with Jesus" (*Steps to Christ,* pp. 81, 82).

Apparently Jesus did not conceive of witnessing as a regimented program with deadlines and statistics. As He entrusted Himself continually to God, His life from day to day was the simple fulfillment of His Father's will. The same applies also to us today in whatever situation we find ourselves. He already knows well the different opportunities we will have each day to witness for Him. In fact, in His love and wisdom He is doing, and will do, everything possible to work out and to help us discern and seize such opportunities.

You see, Christ witnessed on the job. He did not go there necessarily to witness, rather He witnessed as He went. And as He did He discerned needs and grasped opportunities to minister to others along the way. It is interesting to note that most of His encounters with people took place this way. Just study the Gospel of Mark and see how in almost every chapter the writer introduces such encounters with statements such as "when He drew near to," "as He came out of," and "while He was at."

"Wherever He [Jesus] was, in the synagogue, by the way-side, in the boat . . . , at the Pharisee's feast or the table of the publican, He spoke to men of the things pertaining to the higher life. The things of nature, the events of daily life, were bound up by Him with the words of truth. . . . When He opened His lips to speak, their attention was riveted upon Him, and every word was to some soul a savor of life unto life" (*Christ's Object Lessons,* p. 338). Encouraging us to follow Christ's example, Ellen White also explains how we may apply this in our lives as we mingle with others for Him. "Wherever we are, we should watch for opportunities of speaking to others of the Saviour. If we follow Christ's example in doing good, hearts will open to us as they did to Him. Not abruptly, but with tact born of divine love, we can tell them of Him" (*ibid.,* p. 339).

Hans Kung, the well-known German theologian, contends that modern Christians often do not have a clear idea of what it means to be Christ's agents influencing the world around them. Furthermore, he argues that we have drifted away from the early church's understanding of involvement and ministry. The church then did not find itself impeded by sophisticated programs and institutions, but Christ's followers were free to penetrate every aspect of their life and work in society with their witness for Christ (*Why Priests?* pp. 13-15, 17-23).

Martin Luther also affirmed the New Testament concept of witnessing as a way of life. It frustrated him when church members hoarded the blessings of the gospel. He called it "the worst trick of the devil." Luther stressed that serving the Lord does not take place only in "churches but also in the home, kitchen, workshop, field" (in Feucht, *Everyone a Minister,* p. 80).

Christ's method always places the emphasis on faithful men and women who become Jesus' mouth, hands, and heart to others. No matter how superior a program is, it cannot succeed unless we have the right people in place. And that is where God's people find themselves every day of their lives. As His agents they are there unobtrusively invading every sector of life.

Richard Halverson describes such agents as "beachheads of the kingdom, in business, education, government, labor, and the professions." He specifies such beachheads as Christ's cumulative influence in the world. "The authentic impact of Jesus Christ in the world is the collective influence of individual Christians right where they are, day in, day out. Doctors, lawyers, merchants, farmers, teachers, accountants, laborers, students, politicians, athletes, clerks, executives . . . quietly, steadily, continually, consistently infecting the world where they live with a contagious witness of the contemporary Christ and His relevance to life" ("The Tragedy of the Unemployed," *Christianity Today,* Sept. 12, 1960, pp. 9, 10).

Some Christians always assume that real witnessing takes place everywhere else except where they happen to be. And while they think of reaching out to those over there, they neglect to make an impact on those *where they are.* Can you, for example, imagine a Christian in his rush to witness to an atheist out there, walking over the people closest to him—his wife, children, church members, neighbors, work associates?

Or can you imagine someone who, in the process of hurrying to arrive on time for a witnessing workshop, totally ignores the individuals along the way who desperately need his witness. "We need not go to heathen lands, or even leave the narrow circle of the home, if it is there that our duty lies, in order to work for Christ. We can do this in the home circle, in the church, among those with whom we associate, and with whom we do business" (*Steps to Christ,* p. 81).

Thus personal witnessing becomes as integral a part of life as breathing as we make the most of our day-to-day contacts. It is definitely not some kind of venture that we whimsically pick up or abandon. Those we meet during our daily activities form a unique group that no other individual may be able to influence in the same way that we can. Already having at least an idea of who we are, they observe us on a regular basis, thereby progressively developing meaningful relationships. They do not consider it strange for us to talk and exchange ideas with them. And if we do not complete a conversation, there is always another day for follow-up.

Win Arn, of the Institute for American Church Growth, makes such circles of Christian influence his priority concern. In one significant study he conducted on several thousand church members representing different denominations, he asked them to select the factors that influenced them to belong to a church. From 70 to 90 percent of them responded that the friends and relatives they encountered in their daily lives had had the greatest impact on them ("People Are Asking," *Church Growth: America,* March/April 1979, p. 11).

During witnessing workshops I ask the participants, "How many individuals who need your personal witness do you come in contact with in the normal and daily course of your life?" I have discovered that the average church member encounters between 10 and 14 such persons. Imagine the potential impact we have not only on tens of persons, but even hundreds, thousands, and millions. That is why I tell everyone in my witnessing classes and workshops to write down on a piece of paper all the names of individuals in their spheres of influence who need their witness. Then I request them to place the list in their Bibles and to pray for them during their daily worship. They are to consider those 10 to 14 individuals as their special mission project.

It is amazing how things begin to happen when we make ourselves available to God. Doors open before us. It is as if He has been already working on their hearts and arranging circumstances to bring us into contact with them. Such opportunities probably already existed, but we did not yet see people and circumstances from God's perspective. However, when we ally ourselves with God's strategy of saving souls, we discern things anew. And now God sends along our way individuals whom He would not have otherwise, because we are receptive to His leading and working in our lives. We have become His active agents in His divine network and strategy to bring His love and salvation to all around us.

Hank, a Christian accountant who became acquainted with Christ's method, wanted to put it to work at his office. But at the same time he explained that he was bored with his profession, and that he did not think that his work associates were really interested in God or religion. When I asked him to what extent he was acquainted with them, he said that they talked only about superficial things such as the weather and sports. I asked him to write down the names of his colleagues, place them in his Bible, and daily pray for each one of them. Also, I encouraged him to specifically pray that God would lead him to one person, to make one meaningful contact on the job.

As he went to the office that week, nothing out of the ordinary took place, except that he was conscious of the fact that God was active in the hearts of his colleagues. God was also working on him personally, impressing him to silently pray and discern different opportunities. He did not quite expect what happened next. No exceptional opportunity presented itself, just something routine that usually annoyed him. But now it was different, because he was different. Almost every day around lunchtime, Ken, a colleague of his, would pass by Hank's desk, tap his abdomen, and say, "Well, I guess I'm getting hungry. I'm going to get myself something to eat."

The daily habit bothered Hank, but he managed to tolerate it without showing how he really felt. But this particular day, as Ken approached his desk and said the usual thing, Hank asked where Ken usually ate lunch. He wanted to mingle and to take personal interest as Jesus did. His colleague gladly told him. "I'm getting hungry too," Hank commented. "Would you mind if I come along and try out that restaurant?"

"Great, let's go," Ken said, motioning toward the door. "They serve good sandwiches there, and the prices are quite reasonable."

As they sat across the table from each other, they began to exchange different ideas and experiences. They enjoyed visiting together, and were surprised that they had not gotten together earlier, considering that for several years they had been working for the same firm. Two days later they again went out to eat. When he learned that Hank was attending church, Ken expressed some interest because his boys were going through some problems. "For years we have thought of attending church as a family, especially now. But we don't know where to start,'' he explained.

Eventually the two families became friends, and they started to attend church and study the Bible together. Within a few months Ken and his family committed their lives to Christ. The experience made quite a spiritual impact on Hank's life and work. He clearly sensed that God was real and willing to use him. His work became more interesting, and began to have a different dimension. Now he looked forward to going to the office to see how God was going to use him that day. In fact, he and Ken began to pray for the rest of their work associates, and the Lord kept opening doors for them to witness.

Christ declared that while the harvest is ready, only a few of the laborers are prepared to reap it (see Matt. 9:37). Ellen White tells us that there are ''many who need the ministration of loving Christian hearts. Many have gone down to ruin who might have been saved if their neighbors, common men and women, had put forth personal effort for them. Many are waiting to be personally addressed. In the very family, the neighborhood, the town, where we live, there is work for us to do as missionaries for Christ'' (*The Desire of Ages,* p. 141).

So far we have not said much about the number of converts resulting from personal witnessing. We need to emphasize that following Christ will not merely yield a plentiful harvest, but also a quality one. For the way we relate to others in the process of witnessing to them, spiritually nurturing them, and equipping them to minister to others, has a great deal to do with their spiritual vitality and fruitfulness.

Ellen White summarizes Christ's method of witnessing and how we should relate to it: ''If we would humble ourselves before God, and be kind and courteous and tenderhearted and pitiful, there would be one hundred conversions to the truth where now there is only one. But, though professing to be converted, we carry around with us a bundle of self that we regard as altogether too precious to be given up'' (*Testimonies,* vol. 9, p. 189).

BY HIS SPIRIT

It was during the terrible blizzard of February 1899. The streets of Brooklyn were blocked with snow. The streetcars were unable to run. For days no attempt was made to clear any but the great business thoroughfares. I was living on a side street. The snow was waist deep in places on our street, and still it stormed. Our baby girl of 18 months became ill with a burning fever. All night she called for water. She was weak and would not eat, but still was able to walk. The following evening she was lying in her mother's lap. Presently she looked up and said through her parched lips, 'Mama, apple.' My wife looked at me with a pained expression and said, 'Papa, there isn't an apple in the house.'

"The baby heard her and, sliding down from her mother's lap, toddled over to where I sat, and putting one little hand on each of my knees, looked up into my face through her tired blue eyes and said, 'Papa, apple.' She did not think of the impossibilities; she did not look at the storm or the snow. She looked only at papa, and prayed for an apple. A determination came over me, too deep for words, which only could be expressed in works. I immediately arose and, putting on my stormcoat, threw myself into the drifts against the storm. I sometimes waded, and sometimes wallowed, but I was wonderfully happy, happy in the thought of bringing back an apple to reward the faith in that upturned face. And by and by I succeeded, and with added joy I hurried back to the baby" (A. F. Ballenger, *Power for Witnessing,* pp. 149, 150).

In Ballenger's impassioned account of a father's love toward his child, it caused him to brave the raging storm in order to grant her heart's desire. Doesn't it remind us of what Jesus said about our heavenly Father being willing to shower us with good gifts? "What father among you, if his son asks for a fish, will instead of a fish give him a serpent; or if he asks for an egg, will give him a scorpion? If you then, who are evil, know how to give good gifts to your children, how much more will the heavenly Father give the Holy Spirit to those who ask him!" (Luke 11:11-13).

The question we need to ask ourselves is If our Father is so willing to bestow on us the Holy Spirit, why are we so reluctant to ask for and accept the gift? If we expect even evil parents to bring their children food, shelter, and other good things, most certainly we can trust an infinitely loving and good heavenly Father to grant us the Holy Spirit. After all, He has already proved Himself by sending us His only Son (John 3:16). "The promise of the Holy Spirit is casually brought into our discourses, is incidentally touched upon, and that is all. . . . This subject has been set aside, as if some time in the future would be given to its consideration. . . . This promised blessing, if claimed by faith, would bring all other blessings in its train" (*Testimonies to Ministers,* pp. 174, 175).

Perhaps one of the causes for our reluctance to receive the Holy Spirit is the ambiguity or extremism that many Christians feel about the subject. One extreme is seeking the anointing of the Holy Spirit for the purpose of sentimental emotionalism and self-edification. Such an emphasis makes us cautious because we try to avoid fanaticism or counterfeit spiritual behavior. The other danger is becoming so careful about receiving the wrong spirit that we miss the Holy Spirit altogether.

Of course, we must be careful in these last days to discern what is genuine and what is not. We certainly know that Satan will try to deceive even God's elect (Matt. 24:24). But on the other hand, Satan also attempts to make us so cautious and spiritually insensitive that we miss the genuine experience of the

Holy Spirit. He is an expert in deception, and he does not care how he tricks God's people.

What we really need to do is to become so close to Christ that we will have the spiritual perception to help us be balanced in relating to the extremely pivotal relationship between the Holy Spirit and witnessing. For without the Holy Spirit, we simply will not be able to witness for Christ in His way. So it is not a casual concern that we can treat with indifference. "But should the Lord work upon men as He did on and after the day of Pentecost, many who now claim to believe the truth . . . would cry, 'Beware of fanaticism.'. . . There will be those who will question and criticize when the Spirit of God takes possession of men and women, because their own hearts are not moved, but are cold and unimpressible" (*Selected Messages,* book 2, p. 57).

We have repeatedly referred to Christ and His example in witnessing. But we must also emphasize the fact that Jesus manifests Himself to us through the Holy Spirit. The Holy Spirit is the one who gives us the power for witnessing. And without Him we represent only ourselves, not Christ. Without Him our witness becomes self-centered, cold, and devoid of any power. The New Testament inextricably links the Holy Spirit with the sharing of the gospel. However, since Jesus seems to be more real to us, we identify and feel more at ease with Him.

Perhaps we have jumped to the conclusion that the Holy Spirit is just something ethereal, an idea or an influence. But the Scriptures present Him as a functioning person just as the Father and the Son are. In fact, the closeness of the three members of the Godhead is quite apparent in the designation of the Holy Spirit as both "the Spirit of God," and "the Spirit of Christ" in Romans 8:9 (Philip Samaan, *Portraits of the Messiah in Zechariah,* pp. 53, 54).

What then is the relationship between the Holy Spirit and Christ? His work is "linked together with Christ's life and ministry. He was a close companion to Christ from the very beginning. Christ was conceived of the Holy Spirit (Matt. 1:20) and anointed by the Spirit at His baptism, thus commencing Jesus' public ministry (John 1:32-34). The Holy Spirit was sent to fill Christ's place as the other Comforter, and so He is among us as Christ's personal representative (John 14:16-26). He does not speak on His own authority, but He bears witness to Christ and glorifies Him (John 16:13, 14; 15:26)" (*ibid.*, p. 54).

The Holy Spirit's ministry in bearing witness of Christ is intertwined with the Father bearing witness of the Son, and the Son, likewise, witnessing to the Father. Note how we fit in this interwoven web that reveals not self but the Other. Observe also the progressive order of such witness: 1. The Father bears witness of the Son (John 5:30-32, 37). 2. The Son, in turn, testifies of the Father (John 14:8, 9). He is indeed "the true and faithful witness" (Rev. 1:5; 3:14). 3. The Holy Spirit, likewise, points to and represents the Son (John 16:13-15). 4. Finally, we bear witness of Christ through the infilling in us of the Other Witness, the Holy Spirit. He reveals Himself through our witness. "And we are witnesses to these things, and so is the Holy Spirit whom God has given to those who obey him" (Acts 5:32).

Furthermore, it becomes evident to us when we study the four Gospels that the Holy Spirit thoroughly participated in every aspect of Christ's life, especially in His ministry of depicting the Father. John the Baptist testified that the Holy Spirit descended and remained on Jesus at the time of His baptism (Mark 1:12). Consequently, Jesus would then baptize others with the Holy Spirit and with fire (John 1:33; Luke 3:16). Thus His baptism in the Holy Spirit was His consecration for public ministry, which followed immediately (Luke 3:23).

Moreover, Luke reports that Jesus was "full of the Holy Spirit" and that He "was led by the Spirit" (Luke 4:1). Then He returned from the wilderness "in the power of the Spirit" (verse 14), and on the Sabbath He entered the synagogue and read a passage from Isaiah relating to both Himself *and* to the Holy Spirit: "The Spirit of the Lord is upon me, because he has anointed me to preach good news to the poor. He has sent me to proclaim release to the captives and recovering of sight to the blind, to set at liberty those who are oppressed, to proclaim the acceptable year of the Lord" (Luke 4:18, 19).

The passage presents three important aspects of the Holy Spirit's relationship to Jesus. One, the Holy Spirit was present in His life. Two, the Holy Spirit anointed Him. Three, He was anointed by the Spirit to preach good news, to witness, and to minister to people. Therefore, the Father gave the Holy Spirit to Jesus then — and to us today — for the sole purpose of anointing us to serve and to witness to those around us.

Also, the apostle Peter links the anointing of Christ and His service. He makes the connection between how God "anointed Jesus of Nazareth with the Holy Spirit and with power" and how Christ accordingly "went about doing good and healing all that were oppressed by the devil" (Acts 10:38, RSV).

Moreover, Christ emphasized the intimate relationship between receiving the Holy Spirit and witnessing when He promised His disciples: "But you shall receive power when the Holy Spirit has come upon you; and you shall be my witnesses in Jerusalem and in all Judea and Samaria and to the end of the earth" (Acts 1:8). The apostle Paul elaborated on this concept of service when he discussed how God intended the various gifts of the Spirit to build up the members of Christ's body so as to equip them for the role of ministry (Eph. 4:11, 12).

In essence, then, following Christ's example in witnessing is a partnership between the divine and the human: the divine Holy Spirit, and us His human agents. We clearly see such divine-human cooperation in the Holy Spirit moving upon the heart of Philip to go and witness to the Ethiopian. At the same time He had also been preparing the heart of the Ethiopian to gladly receive Philip's testimony (see Acts 8:26-35). It should greatly encourage us to know that the Holy Spirit eagerly wants to involve us in His network of reaching out to specific individuals all around us — individuals He has already been preparing for us. How many times has the Holy Spirit attempted to use us in specific situations when, unfortunately, we are not in tune with Him?

How can we ever think that we can powerfully bear witness to Christ without the infilling of the Holy Spirit? Sometimes we give the impression that some of the church business and evangelistic programs can operate without the total control of the Holy Spirit. And in our preoccupation with managing God's work, puffed up with our own wisdom and proficiency, we may not even recognize the absence of the Holy Spirit. A friend one time commented about a skillful and "successful" church leader, "Whenever I hear him speak, or see him at work, he conveys the clear impression that he can manage quite well without prayer or the Holy Spirit."

John Seamands, a veteran missionary, underscores the utter necessity of the Holy Spirit in our witnessing. "As modern communicators of the Word, how we need the fullness and power of the Holy Spirit in our lives! Pentecost is not a spiritual luxury; it is an utter necessity for Christian service. It is not an adornment, but essential equipment; not something we can take or leave as we like, but a must. We are shut up to the alternative: Pentecost or failure. For the human spirit fails unless the Holy Spirit fills" (*Tell It Well,* p. 120).

Great talents and skills, if not surrendered to God, can block the work of the Holy Spirit in our lives. The Holy Spirit cannot fill a full vessel, only an empty one. He simply cannot use even golden vessels if they are rigid and brimming with self. However, He greatly needs clay vessels that are pliable and empty of self. Spending some years in Africa as a missionary, I was amazed to see how the Holy Spirit mightily used simple men and women who had little education, skill, or equipment. Some whom I met were illiterate and extremely poor, but they would reach out in love to others around them, and share with them their testimony and the many Bible texts they had committed to memory. In the process they would win hundreds for God's kingdom. Why? Because they had one great factor going for them: The power of the Holy Spirit was molding their empty vessels and filling them with His power to witness. It is so true that "there is no limit to the usefulness of one who, putting self aside, makes room for the working of the Holy Spirit upon his heart" (*The Ministry of Healing,* p. 159).

Even Moses might have felt that his work for God was as worthless as a handful of common sand or a dry desert bush when the Lord first called him (see Ex. 3 and 4). Moses felt incapable of being used by God. However, even if we feel like all we have to offer God is a handful of common sand, in His presence it becomes holy ground. And a dry bush before God becomes an unlimited fire. The crucial issue is not so much our ability without Him, but our availability to Him. Nothing can transform common sand or the lifeless bush as can the Lord's holiness and the power of His Spirit.

We simply need to give Him just what we have. No more, no less. That is all that He asks us for. He even makes use of our meager talents without needing to bypass our individuality. Remember, God's fire did not consume the bush. So God wants to use us, not to destroy us, in His service. "I would not suggest that surrender to Him [God] sets aside our personality," write Fish and Conant. "He empowers our personality and uses just what we are and have. The power of the [watch's] mainspring does not change the hairspring; it uses it. . . . So also does the indwelling Christ with us" (*Every-Member Evangelism,* p. 97).

But we must not wait any longer to thirst for and be filled with the Holy Spirit. He gives Himself to us not for self, but for service. Therefore, in the very act of submitting ourselves in service to Him, He comes to empower us to witness. "I was shown God's people waiting for some change to take place—a compelling power to take hold of them. But they will be disappointed. . . . They must act; they must take hold of the work themselves, and earnestly cry to God for a true knowledge of the work" (*Christian Service,* p. 82).

Neal C. Wilson, in pondering what the last decade of the twentieth century holds for God's people, has urgently appealed to them to seek the infilling of the Holy Spirit in their lives. He stresses that unless we have the Spirit of God activating our lives, our witness remains feeble and ineffective. In recognizing God's blessing to the church in its evangelistic advance, he states that "the results are minuscule compared to what He longs to enable us to do" through the outpouring of His Spirit upon us. Sensing the crucial need for the outpouring of the Spirit now, Wilson writes: "I must confess that in spite of progress and victories in so many areas, I have become increasingly persuaded that something is lacking. We are not fully measuring up to God's glorious expectations for each of us and for His church" ("Time for Revival," *Adventist Review,* Jan. 4, 1990, p. 2).

Many among God's people act as if a lack of the Holy Spirit is only a theoretical problem we might face in the future. But that lets Satan lull us to sleep and postpone our present need of preparing ourselves, to some later time when it would be too late. God is eager to ready us now to receive the Holy Spirit. Therefore, we need to seek Him, pray for Him, and have Him now (see *Evangelism,* p. 701).

For as we act in faith, reaching out to the needy ones all around us, the Holy Spirit, the mighty angels, and all the powers of Heaven are there to assist us. In sending Jesus to redeem humanity, He has proved that He is willing to give anything and everything to work through us to save the lost. "All Heaven is in activity, and the angels of God are waiting to cooperate with all who will devise plans whereby souls for whom Christ died may hear the glad tidings of salvation" (*Christian Service,* p. 259).

Ellen White describes how the Holy Spirit will mightily use multitudes in witnessing. "Hundreds and thousands were seen visiting families and opening before them the Word of God. Hearts were convicted by the power of the Holy Spirit, and a spirit of genuine conversion was manifest. On every side doors were thrown open to the proclamation of the truth. The world seemed to be lightened with the heavenly influence" (*Testimonies,* vol. 9, p. 126).

Some years back a friend of mine and I had the opportunity of witnessing to a young married couple. It was most rewarding to experience Christ's method in the process of visiting and sharing with them. They accepted Jesus as their Saviour and Lord, and were quite eager to start studying the Bible in their home. Week after week as we pursued the studies, they showed great interest and accepted the teachings we presented from the Scriptures. However, a few months later they would not accept our invitation to commit their lives to Christ in baptism. For several weeks we visited with them, trying to answer their questions and excuses, but to no avail. They simply were determined not to be baptized.

At that time a small group of church members began to meet regularly and to pray that the Holy Spirit would soften the hearts of the man and his wife. The next time we went to their home, we were prepared for their arguments. But to our surprise, they had none whatsoever. In fact, they desired to know when they could be baptized and join the body of Christ. When we asked them what had changed their attitude, they said that they had strongly sensed the Spirit of God all during that week tugging at their hearts to submit themselves completely to Christ.

More than ever before I sense the crucial importance of intercessory prayer in implementing Christ's method of witnessing. I used to wonder how effective such prayer really was. After all, God already loves people, He sent His only Son to die for them, and He is constantly trying to save them. So what part does intercessory prayer play in their salvation? Are we telling God to do something He is already fully committed to do?

First of all, we must remember that Christ Himself is the great petitioner. We also need to follow His example in interceding for others in our prayers to God. The author of the book of Hebrews describes Him as ever living to intercede on behalf of people (Heb. 7:25). Also, the Holy Spirit aids us in our prayers, and joins Christ in making intercession for us before the Father. "Likewise the Spirit helps us in our weakness; for we do not know how to pray as we ought, but the Spirit himself intercedes for us with sighs too deep for words" (Rom. 8:26).

Luke 22:31, 32 records that Jesus prayed for Peter so that he might withstand Satan's assaults against him. Ponder Jesus' moving words to the disciple: "Simon, Simon, behold, Satan demanded to have you, that he might sift you like wheat, but I have prayed for you that your faith may not fail." Do we remember the times we promise to pray for someone only to ignore it or forget all about it?

Christ never forgets us and the struggles we face, but prays for us just as He did for Peter. Ellen White writes that Christ was "Himself a source of blessing and strength, He could heal the sick and raise the dead . . . ; yet He prayed, often with strong crying and tears. He prayed for His disciples and for Himself, thus identifying Himself with human beings. He was a mighty petitioner. As the Prince of life, He had power with God, and prevailed" (*Gospel Workers*, p. 256).

The question is How may we become effective petitioners like Christ? The apostle James admonishes us to remember to pray for one another, for "the prayer of a righteous man has great power in its effects'' (James 5:16). Here we see two important aspects of intercessory prayer: its quality, and its result. Such prayer is earnest and righteous, and it brings about great and powerful results. Christ is a mighty petitioner because He is righteousness. And as His witnesses, who submit ourselves completely to Him, we become righteous in His righteousness, for He is our righteousness (Jer. 23:6), and in Him we become the righteousness of God (2 Cor. 5:21). That is the only way our intercessory prayers can avail in behalf of those to whom we witness.

As we pray for the salvation of others we must never give up easily, but must remain determined and persevering. ''In times past there were those who fastened their minds upon one soul after another, saying, 'Lord, help me to save this soul.' But now such instances are rare. How many act as if they realized the perils of sinners?'' (*ibid.,* p. 65). Moreover, ''Let the workers grasp the promises of God, saying, '. . . I must have this soul converted to Jesus Christ' '' (*Medical Ministry,* p. 244).

Let us look at the experience of Jacob as He wrestled with God. He knew what it meant to strive with God. ''I will not let you go,'' he insisted, ''unless you bless me'' (Gen. 32:26). ''Jacob prevailed because he was persevering and determined. His victory is an evidence of the power of importunate prayer. All who will lay hold of God's promises, as he did, and be as earnest and persevering as he was, will succeed as he succeeded. Those who are unwilling to deny self, to agonize before God, to pray long and earnestly for His blessing, will not obtain it. Wrestling with God—how few know what it is! How few have ever had their souls drawn out after God with intensity of desire until every power is on the stretch'' (*The Great Controversy,* p. 621).

In the parable of the widow pleading her case before an unrighteous judge (Luke 18:1-7), Christ clearly teaches the value of perseverance. Even though the judge did not care at all for the widow, he finally responded to her persistent pleas simply to rid himself of her. If such an uncaring judge finally responds just to avoid being annoyed, would not the righteous Judge ''vindicate his elect, who cry to him day and night? Will he delay long over them?'' "I tell you," Jesus answers His question, "he will vindicate them speedily" (verses 6-8). In other words, if even an evil judge responded to perseverance, how infinitely more our loving and caring God will answer our committed prayers in behalf of those He died for.

Why do we need to persevere so intently in our petitions before God? Is it to convince Him of our need? No, He already knows all things, and He is already convinced that lost souls need to be saved. Let us consider two reasons: One, it teaches us the valuable lesson of totally depending on God and relinquishing ourselves completely to Him. In addition, God also wants to determine if we are really genuine and serious about what we are requesting. He knows that we do not truly appreciate something unless we earnestly seek for it.

Two, in the context of the great conflict between good and evil, where Christ and Satan contend for human hearts and minds, our intercessory prayers allow God to more actively participate in a situation than He would otherwise. In other words, God can answer Satan's objections and justify His special intervention in behalf of the object of our prayer by presenting our petitions as giving Him an invitation to act. Thereby, He is simply honoring our choice in inviting Him to intercede.

Wayne McDill argues that we, as disciples of Christ, are responsible for leading a fellow human being to Christ, and "we have the right to press the legitimate claims of Christ in his life." Then he emphasizes that "prayer is a matter of pressing the legitimate right of Jesus to rule in every life," since He died for every person in the world (*Making Friends for Christ*, p. 92). What happens, then, when we pray to God to move someone's heart? Does He change His mind and go along with our request? Wouldn't He, in His great love, have done that anyway? What difference does it really make? After all, we are sure of His loving attitude toward people in "not wishing that any should perish, but that all should reach repentance" (2 Peter 3:9).

McDill explains again that when you pray for someone to be saved, "remember that you are not trying to convince God. He is already convinced. You are putting yourself in line with His wishes in your prayer. By the authority of Christ take your rightful stand in your neighbor's life and exercise your faith in opening that territory to the extension of kingdom authority. Insist that the enemy retreat in the face of the rightful authority of Christ. . . . Realize that the real battle will be won in prayer'' (*ibid.*, pp. 96, 97).

John Henry Jowett, a deeply spiritual man of God, described the effectiveness of intercessory prayer when he said, "Every time we pray we cut a channel for the energies of grace to flow out towards the object of our prayer'' (Arthur Porritt, in *John Henry Jowett,* pp. 262, 263). And Charles Finney, who knew firsthand the great results of prayers offered by a righteous man, affirmed that "prayer is not to change God, but to change us. Prayer produces such a change in us, and fulfills such conditions in us as to render it consistent for God to do as it would not be consistent for Him to do otherwise'' (Richard E. Day, *Man of Like Passions,* pp. 126, 127).

John Wesley, in emphasizing how effective our sincere petitions are before God, made the radical comment "God does nothing but in answer to prayer'' (cited in Harold L. Calkins, *Master Preachers,* p. 130). What about the effectiveness of Elijah's petition to God on Mount Carmel recorded in 1 Kings 18:36-40? Would God have wrought that mighty miracle if he had not prayed? ''The call of the hour is for men and women who are mighty in prayer, masters of supplication, specialists in the holy art of intercession. The God of Elijah was the answering God. Something happened when Elijah prayed that would not have happened if he had not prayed'' (*ibid.*, p. 137).

The apostle Paul pleads with us to intercede in behalf of all people so that they might respond to God. "First of all, then, I urge that supplications, prayers, intercessions, and thanksgivings be made for all men. . . . This is good, and it is acceptable in the sight of God our Savior, who desires all men to be saved and to come to the knowledge of the truth'' (1 Tim. 2:1-4). Often we talk about prayer, but how often do we really pray? If we honestly examine our lives, do we find ourselves praying for the salvation of specific individuals on a consistent basis? Do we have a burden and passion for souls? How much time do we spend interceding in behalf of a lost humanity? Do we spend five, ten, twenty minutes, if any, in intercessory prayer every day? Christ's ministry, the apostles' witnessing, and the early church's evangelistic advance were immersed in intercessory prayer.

Armin Gesswein in his study of prayer as it intimately relates to witnessing, said, "Prayer is the lifeline of New Testament evangelism, the oxygen for its holy fire. The New Testament was born in prayer. It knows no evangelism without prayer, and no prayer which does not lead to evangelism. God has joined these together in one piece, and no man must separate them" (Armin R. Gesswein, in McDill, p. 88, emphasis supplied).

How can we even imagine that we can witness without it! It is what Satan fears the most. "Satan dreads nothing but prayer," writes Chadwick. "The one concern of the devil is to keep the church from praying. He fears nothing from prayerless studies, prayerless works. . . . He laughs at our toil, mocks our wisdom, but trembles when we pray" (cited in Calkins, p. 129).

One of the most potent results of being filled with the Holy Spirit is the powerful and holy atmosphere with which He surrounds us wherever we are. Each one of us has a certain aura that envelops us. Our circles of influence intersect those of all we interact with. If Christ through the Holy Spirit abides in us, our lives will breathe love and spiritual vitality. On the other hand, if we are filled with ourselves, they discharge a cold and self-centered atmosphere.

We seldom discuss this important aspect of witnessing, but we all experience feelings of being drawn to, repulsed from, or ambivalence about the persons we come in contact with each day. And they experience similar reactions to us. This silent, yet potent form of communication can either enhance our witness or greatly weaken it—and we are often not even aware of the fact. But let there be no mistake about it—whoever actuates our lives, be that the Spirit or self, will be revealed. And that revelation will either confirm or deny our spiritual claims.

"Every soul is surrounded by an atmosphere of its own—an atmosphere, it may be, charged with the life-giving power of faith, courage, and hope, and sweet with the fragrance of love. Or it may be heavy and chill with the gloom of discontent and selfishness, or poisonous with the deadly taint of cherished sin.

By the atmosphere surrounding us, every person with whom we come in contact is consciously or unconsciously affected'' (*Christ's Object Lessons*, p. 339).

This powerful atmosphere of love and spiritual vitality comes only from the indwelling of the Holy Spirit. We have already seen that in our discussion of our being the salt, the light, and the aroma of Christ. Ellen White depicts this atmosphere as "vital energy" (*Thoughts From the Mount of Blessing*, p. 36). "The sincere believers diffuse vital energy, which is penetrating and imparts new moral power to the souls for whom they labor. It is not the power of the man himself, but the power of the Holy Spirit that does the transforming work" (*ibid.*).

How can this book on Christ's method of witnessing possibly conclude without focusing on how Christ exuded such a loving, powerful, and holy atmosphere around Him? He was anointed and actuated by the power of the Holy Spirit. Our lives must be too. We have many needs when it comes to witnessing effectively for Christ. However, our most urgent one in these last days is to be more like Jesus in all things. "A revival of true godliness among us is the greatest and most urgent of all our needs. To seek this should be our first work" (*Selected Messages*, book 1, p. 121). Such spiritual experience with Christ is "the effectual preparation for all who labor for God." Hence, in the middle of the hustle and bustle of life, Christ's disciple "will be surrounded with an atmosphere of light and peace. The life will breathe out fragrance, and will reveal a divine power that will reach men's hearts" (*The Desire of Ages*, p. 363).

Dear reader, do you truly want to be like Christ in your life? Do you yearn to reflect His character in your daily witness? Then I entreat you to prayerfully meditate with me on these inspired and life-changing words about our supreme example of witnessing, Jesus Christ.

"But as the people looked upon Him [Jesus], they saw a face where divine compassion was blended with conscious power. Every glance of the eye, every feature of the countenance, was marked with humility, and expressive of unutterable love. He seemed to be surrounded by an atmosphere of spiritual influence" (*ibid.*, pp. 137, 138). "Oh, what rays of softness and beauty shone forth in the daily life of our Saviour! What sweetness flowed from His very presence! The same spirit will be revealed in His children. Those with whom Christ dwells will be surrounded with a divine atmosphere'' (*Thoughts From the Mount of Blessing,* p. 135).

———

BIBLIOGRAPHY

Books

Ballenger, A. F. *Power for Witnessing.* Minneapolis: Dimension Books, 1963.

Bonhoeffer, Dietrich. *The Cost of Discipleship.* New York: Macmillan Pub., 1976.

_____ . *Life Together.* New York: Harper and Brothers, 1954.

Calkins, Harold L. *Master Preachers.* Alma Park, Great Britain: Stanborough Press Ltd., 1986.

Coleman, Robert E. *The Master Plan of Evangelism.* Old Tappan, N. J.: Fleming H. Revel Co., 1980.

Conn, Harvey M. *Evangelism.* Grand Rapids: Zondervan Pub. House, 1982.

Cooper, Douglas. *Living God's Love.* Mountain View, Calif.: Pacific Press Pub., 1975.

Day, Richard E. *Man of Like Passions.* Grand Rapids: Zondervan Pub. House, 1942.

DeVille, Jard. *The Psychology of Witnessing.* Waco, Tex.: Word Books, 1980.

Feucht, Oscar E. *Everyone a Minister.* St. Louis: Concordia Pub. House, 1976.

Fish, Roy J. and J. E. Conant. *Every-Member Evangelism.* New York: Harper and Row, 1976.

Gesswein, Armin R. *Evangelism the Next Ten Years.* Ed. Sherwood E. Wirt. Waco, Tex.: Word Books, 1978.

Jauncey, James H. *One-on-One Evangelism.* Chicago: Moody Press, 1979.

BIBLIOGRAPHY

Keefauver, Larry. *Friends and Faith*. Loveland, Colo.: Group Books, 1986.

Keller, Phillip W. *Salt for Society*. Waco, Tex.: Word Books, 1981.

Knowles, George E. *How to Help Your Church Grow*. Washington, D.C.: Review and Herald Pub., 1981.

Kromminga, Carl G. *Bringing God's News to Neighbors*. Nutley, N.J.: Presbyterian Pub. Co., 1975.

Kung, Hans. *Why Priests?* Garden City, N.Y.: Doubleday and Co., 1972.

Larson, Bruce. *Ask Me to Dance*. Waco, Tex.: Word Books, 1972.

Laymon, Charles M., ed. *The Interpreter's One-Volume Commentary on the Bible*. Nashville: Abingdon Press, 1984.

Little, Paul E. *How to Give Away Your Faith*. Chicago: InterVarsity Press, 1966.

Maslow, Abraham. *Motivation and Personality*. New York: Harper and Row, 1970.

McDill, Wayne. *Making Friends for Christ*. Nashville: Broadman Press, 1979.

McPhee, Arthur G. *Friendship Evangelism*. Grand Rapids: Zondervan Pub. House, 1978.

Miles, Delos. *Overcoming Barriers to Witnessing*. Nashville: Broadman Press, 1984.

Miller, Keith. *A Second Touch*. Waco, Tex.: Word Books, 1974.

Neighbour, Ralph. *Witness, Take the Stand*. Dallas: Baptist General Convention of Texas Publications, 1967.

Ortiz, Juan Carlos. *Disciple*. Carol Stream, Ill.: Creation House, 1978.

Pippert, Rebecca Manley. *Out of the Saltshaker*. Downers Grove, Ill.: InterVarsity Press, 1979.

Ponder, James A., ed. *Motivating Laymen to Witness*. Nashville: Broadman Press, 1974.

Prince, Matthew. *Winning Through Caring*. Grand Rapids: Baker Book House, 1981.

Porritt, Arthur. *John Henry Jowett*. Garden City, N.Y.: Doubleday and Co., 1925.

Rand, Ron. *Won by One*. Ventura, Calif.: Regal Books, 1988.

Richards, Lawrence O. *Youth Ministry*. Grand Rapids: Zondervan Pub. House, 1985.

Samaan, Philip G. *Portraits of the Messiah in Zechariah*. Hagerstown, MD.: Review and Herald Pub., 1989.

Schoen, V. W. *God's Need*. Washington, D.C.: Review and Herald Pub., 1976.

Seamands, John T. *Tell It Well*. Kansas City, Mo.: Beacon Hill Press of Kansas City, 1981.

Stedman, Ray C. *Body Life*. Glendale, Calif.: Regal Books, 1976.

Stott, John R. W. *Basic Christianity*. Grand Rapids: William B. Eerdmans Pub. Co., 1986.

Sweeting, George. *How to Witness Successfully*. Chicago: Moody Press, 1978.

The Seventh-day Adventist Bible Commentary. Ed. F. D. Nichol. Washington, D.C.: Review and Herald Pub. Assn., 1953-1957.

Tournier, Paul. *The Meaning of Persons*. New York: Harper and Row, 1957.

Watson, David. *I Believe in Evangelism*. Grand Rapids: William B. Eerdmans Pub. Co., 1979.

White, Ellen G. *The Acts of the Apostles*. Mountain View, Calif.: Pacific Press Pub. Assn., 1911.

_____ . *Christ's Object Lessons*. Mountain View, Calif.: Pacific Press Pub. Assn., 1941.

_____ . *Christian Service*. Washington, D.C.: General Conference of SDA, 1947.

_____ . *Counsels to Parents and Teachers*. Mountain View, Calif.: Pacific Press Pub. Assn., 1943.

_____ . *The Desire of Ages*. Mountain View, Calif.: Pacific Press Pub. Assn., 1940.

_____ . *Education*. Mountain View, Calif.: Pacific Press Pub. Assn., 1952.

_____ . *Evangelism*. Washington, D.C.: Review and Herald Pub. Assn., 1946.

_____ . *Gospel Workers*. Washington, D.C.: Review and Herald Pub. Assn., 1948.

BIBLIOGRAPHY

_____ . *The Great Controversy*. Mountain View, Calif.: Pacific Press Pub. Assn., 1950.

_____ . *Medical Ministry*. Mountain View, Calif.: Pacific Press Pub. Assn., 1963.

_____ . *The Ministry of Healing*. Mountain View, Calif.: Pacific Press Pub. Assn., 1942.

_____ . *Selected Messages*. Washington, D.C.: Review and Herald Pub. Assn., 1958.

_____ . *Steps to Christ*. Washington, D.C.: Review and Herald Pub. Assn., 1908.

_____ . *Testimonies for the Church*. Mountain View, Calif.: Pacific Press Pub. Assn., 1948.

_____ . *Testimonies to Ministers and Gospel Workers*. Mountain View, Calif.: Pacific Press Pub. Assn., 1962.

_____ . *Thoughts From the Mount of Blessing*. Mountain View, Calif.: Pacific Press Pub. Assn., 1956.

Periodicals

Arn, Win. "People Are Asking." *Church Growth: America,* March/April 1979.

Drescher, John M. "A Fish Story." *Ministry,* April 1979.

"God, I Want to Live!" *Time,* June 2, 1980.

Halverson, Richard C. "The Tragedy of the Unemployed." *Christianity Today,* Sept. 12, 1960.

Holland, Kenneth J. "Truth Must Also Move the Heart." *These Times,* September 1980.

Jaecks, Lenard D. "Adventists Involved in the 'Shut Door' Again." *Gleaner,* Dec. 18, 1989.

Johnsson, William G. "The Missing Tell Us Why." *Adventist Review,* Sept. 7, 1989.

Littleton, Mark R. "The Fine Art of Encouragement." *Reader's Digest,* November 1989.

Sahlin, Monte. "Where Are Our Missing Members?" *Adventist Review,* May 4, 1989.

Seeliger, Wes. in *Faith at Work,* February 1972.

Stimson, Henry L. "The Bomb and the Opportunity." *Harper's Magazine,* March 1946.

Taylor, Daniel. "The Fear of Insignificance." *Signs of the Times*, November 1989.

Widmer, Myron. "My Friends, the 'Missing.' " *Adventist Review*, May 4, 1989.

Wilson, Neal C. "Time for Revival." *Adventist Review*, Jan. 4, 1990.